Weight off y
plate

By Lynda Roberts

DEDICATION

I would like to dedicate this book to all of my successful weight loss clients who have turned their lives around. May you always be slim, beautiful and full of confidence!

ISBN-13: 978-0-9954599-4-6

Published by Ann Jaloba Publishing, 26 Tapton Mount Close, Sheffield S10 5DJ

Note to Readers

The information, including opinion and analysis contained herein are based on the author's personal experiences and is not engaged in rendering medical advice or professional services. The information provided herein should not be used for diagnosing or treating a health problem or disease. It is not a substitute for professional care. Readers are advised to consult a doctor for medical advice before commencing any exercise regimen or lifestyle change programme. The author and the publisher make no warranties, either expressed or implied, concerning the accuracy, applicability, activeness, reliability or suitability of the contents. If you wish to apply or follow the advice or recommendations mentioned herein, you take full responsibility for your actions. The author and the publisher of this book shall in no event be held liable for any direct, indirect, incidental or other consequential damages arising directly or indirectly from any use of the information contained in this book. All content is for information only and is not warranted for content accuracy or any other implied or explicit purpose.

CONTENTS

INTRODUCTION:

Hello and welcome to this little book of information and suggestions to help you use the power of your mind to permanently reduce your weight and raise your confidence, without the need for calorie counting, or depriving yourself of the taste of your favourite food!

This book is for those ladies who want to lose weight and increase their confidence and self-esteem. For those ladies who are large, gorgeous and loving it I salute you, you are all beautiful!

Whatever your size and shape now, there is a gorgeous slim and sassy woman inside, and you could be meeting her in the very near future! You can be that confident, slim woman with high self-esteem and a 'Can do' attitude to life.

My name is Lynda Roberts, and among all my other titles in life I am a Clinical Hypnotherapist and Trainer. I have been in practice since 2007, and since then have gone on to train many other hypnotherapists from all walks of life. Before training as a hypnotherapist I was a body work therapist and trainer for 10 years, offering a wide range of therapies, including Nutritional Advice.

Although I work with all areas of hypnotherapy, I specialise in motivational weight loss, because it's a subject I'm really passionate about. I can honestly say I love my work and seeing someone change from being fat and unhappy to smiling and even laughing at the way they used to respond to situations and food is more rewarding than retail therapy. As a woman you'll know that puts it top of the tree!

The aim of the book is to help you understand why you may feel anxious and emotional at a subconscious level, and how anxiety and overeating are very closely linked. I want to give you the knowledge and skills to take back control of your anxiety and eating habits, revealing the confident, happy person that you really are. I'll explain how the brain likes to keep repeating the same responses to situations in your life, and how to recognise your own personal triggers to overeating.

We all lead very busy lives, and some degree of anxiety is very natural and necessary. When the anxiety becomes a long term way of life, sometimes it spills over into stress and even depression.

Food is a natural comforter, but when the weight piles on in addition to the negative feelings, the mountain can seem very high indeed! Your confidence disappears along with your self-esteem, and before you know it, you've pushed the repeat button on that never ending cycle of anxiety-eating for comfort-feeling guilty-reinforcing low self-esteem-craving unhealthy foods, and it feels as though you're on a fast moving merry-go-round with no way to get off. But there is a way, and I will show you!

I will give you strategies to break that habitual cycle of anxiety-eat-guilt-anxiety, which in turn will give you a real sense of control over everything in your life that you can control – responses to stress and food choices are definitely within your control to change! Once you've mastered that little trick, your gorgeous, slim and sassy self can emerge! She hasn't disappeared, just been mislaid for a while, but now it's time to bring her back!

The first chapters are there to give you knowledge about how your brain works in relation to anxiety and overeating. It's important that you understand how even such a seemingly innocent substance as sugar can change your mood in a heartbeat, bringing that feel good feeling crashing to the floor.

I will also be giving you some examples of successful clients who have become slimmer, healthier and more confident by embracing a new lifestyle and respect for themselves. It is so often the case that once food is used to fill the void in an emotionally charged mind, as the weight gets higher the self-esteem falls lower, as food is used as a temporary escape route. Using the techniques and tips in this book will help you to gain a new respect for not only yourself, but the food that you choose to eat. Change your mindset and you can change your size, shape and levels of the feel good factor, so that you can enjoy a sense of calm confidence – and control!

I'll share my own personal story with you, to show that no matter how much it feels as if there's no way you can change your life, there always is. Emotional eating is rarely about simply overeating, it's about the need to be comforted or compensated for something that's not right in your world.

Once you have digested (no pun intended!) the first chapters, it's on to how you can change from being a fat person with no confidence, low self-esteem and poor self-image to that beautiful woman you really are. When you feel confident, you ooze confidence and others are drawn to you. They want to know the secret of your sparkling eyes and clear skin. They admire the way you walk with a great posture and head held high, because you are staking your place in the world!

The book is your support and guidance, so make good use of it, roll up your sleeves, and start taking back control!

Here's to a slim and sassy new you!

Best wishes,

Lynda

Who will be reading this book?

"I am someone who has struggled with weight loss for a long time. I have tried every diet and always ended up putting on more weight once the diet has stopped, which makes me feel negative about myself. I know I make excuses constantly and need a way to achieve permanent weight loss, without feeling restricted. When I spoke to Lynda about her book and motivational weight loss programme I was so excited! I will be the first to buy the book and tell all my friends about it. I know Lynda is really experienced in helping people lose weight so once I've read the book I'll definitely be looking at joining the six week programme. This is what I've been waiting for!"

Sharon Hall, Ipswich.

"Keeping and maintaining my weight has been an ongoing battle. Upon meeting Lynda, she explained her motivational permanent weight loss book and 6 week programme to me. I am super excited to be finally able to purchase and read her book containing real life information which allows me to deal with my weight loss issues permanently. I will be the first to purchase her book and spread her invaluable information. Finding Lynda was simply like a breath of fresh air."

Denise Bywaters, Colchester

Chapter One

UNDERSTANDING HOW YOUR BRAIN WORKS

In order to understand how parts of your brain affect your eating, I am going to outline briefly the parts of the brain and what they do. Not too much psycho-babble, I promise! The human brain has three parts which communicate directly with one another, and are linked in with our behaviours, instincts and decision-making.

The Lizard Brain

The first brains appeared in worms around 500 million years ago, and we still have this brain part, known as the Reptilian or Lizard Brain. Not a particularly inviting name! This is the most primitive part of the brain, located deep inside the structure, and extending up from the brain stem. It has no thinking or rational abilities; it simply acts on instinct and runs automated systems within the body such as breathing, heart rate and balance. You're not consciously aware of this part of your brain.

The Limbic System

The next part of the brain, the paleo mammalian, or old mammalian brain, evolved around 250 million years ago. In us, this part of the brain is known as the limbic system. It is divided into four communication parts:

- The hypothalamus, which monitors the stress response
- The amygdala, which recognises anxiety and fear, resulting in the fight or flight response
- The cingulate gyrus, which links smells and sights with memories, emotions connected to pain, and also regulates levels of aggression
- The hippocampus, which is concerned with memory storage

The limbic system is responsible for feeding, fighting, running away and sexual reproduction. It is the centre for our emotions, together with higher mental functions such as learning and formation of memories.

The heritage of the limbic system

When man started to evolve, the primitive brain centres were all there was. He had no way of thinking about his actions, or making any decisions based on thought, he just did what came naturally. As his environment would have been a dangerous one, man needed to have a split second alert to danger, and the aggression to see the danger off (or kill it). The heritage of this today is your instinctive responses from your limbic system: instinctive rather than emotional or rational.

The thinking brain

Then came the pre-frontal cortex, the thinking brain we have today. This part of the brain evolved around 200 million years ago, and is the part of our brain where we make decisions, plan and apply logic and rationale to our decisions and actions.

This part of the brain also interprets sensory input. When we think about our responses and actions, we do so in the pre frontal cortex. When we have an immediate, no-thought urgent response, it comes from the limbic system.

Making sense so far?

So, the primitive brain deals with anxiety, stress, anger, aggression and survival. As we need to eat to survive, this part of the brain creates the need for instant gratification, particularly in times of emotional upheaval, as part of the survival instinct. Food is a necessity, stress and anxiety are a normal part of our lives short term, and when we are stressed, we are responding with the same part of the brain that gives us the urge to eat to survive.

Instinctive response

It makes sense therefore, that when you are feeling anxious, bored, lonely, angry, upset or just downright fed up, food becomes a comforting sedative. The drive to overeat, or reach for the nearest food without thought of nutritional value comes from your limbic system. It is instinctive, just as a baby needs instant gratification when upset or hungry. Food placates the anxious feelings, and that temporarily feels good. Eating, particularly foods high in simple carbohydrates or sugars, can be very pleasurable at the time, and is often used as short term reward or compensation for negative feelings.

When you're feeling relaxed, it's the pre-frontal cortex, or thinking part of the brain, that decides what to eat by planning your nutritional intake based on logic and choice.

Primitive eating

The primitive brain evolved to suit the needs of our ancestors, but is still very much in use in our modern lives. Primitive man's brain meant he ate in a manner that just might be construed as impolite these days. So let's take a more detailed look.

Survival and eating

This is how it used to be. Kill or be killed. If it's chasing you, kill it and eat it – or get away from it as quickly as possible. (Unlikely to happen in a restaurant) There were no emotions or thoughts. No 'what shall we have for dinner tonight?'. Hungry, need food, kill food, eat food. Job done. Primitive man lived on high alert due to his environment, and as the only part of his brain was the primitive survival part, meditation and calmness just didn't come into it.

Primitive man needed to keep the human race going, and without food and sexual reproduction, that wouldn't have happened – again courtesy of the primitive brain that we all still have. Man needed fuel to reproduce, and also needed to eliminate any threats to his mating procedures.

Primitive man needed fuel in order to survive his environment, with no time (or brain power) to plan, so instant gratification was the only way to get it.

When food was available, it was eaten with huge voracity, as someone or something else could come along at any second and take the food (and maybe kill man into the bargain). Animals still do this, as they don't have the pre frontal cortex part that we have to be able to rationalise. Notice how territorial and urgent your dog or cat is the next time you feed him.

Your brain and eating

When you're stressed and anxious, your amygdala instructs your adrenals to pump out adrenaline to give you the power surge to fight or run away. Of course these days, there is usually very little actually to run away from, but an imagined threat produces the same response in the brain to one that is real, and that is when you might be turning to food for comfort due to the anxious feelings. The language of the amygdala is emotion, not words. When you experience an amygdala-based memory, you experience it directly as the emotional state. When you experience memories with the pre-frontal cortex, you see it with images. When you plan a meal, you're doing it with images, perhaps imagining yourself shopping for the ingredients, or reading a recipe book or doing a Google search.

You might see the faces of the people who will be enjoying the meal. You can even conjure up the taste and smell of the food just by imagining it! So many images are associated with planning, all of which are produced in the pre-frontal cortex, or thinking brain.

Eating when stressed: what happens

When you're stressed and anxious, you reach for comfort food, usually food that doesn't require much, if any, preparation or thought – remember the instant gratification that is needed by the primitive brain?

You eat fast, without paying any attention to what you're eating – even if it's chocolate! Remember the primitive brain hasn't changed since early man, so the food will be eaten as if it would disappear if not consumed quickly, even though food is plentiful in our modern western world. The signal that the body is comfortably full doesn't have a chance to reach the brain before over eating has taken place, due to the speed of ingestion. You will probably be familiar with the term 'mindfulness'. Eating without thought is the opposite – 'mindlessness'.

The guilt cycle

Once the food frenzy is over, guilt sets in, together with self-loathing. I'm not suggesting it's the same for everyone; I'm referring to people who are gripped in that cycle of anxiety-eat-guilt-anxiety. The feelings of guilt and shame that follow over eating or even eating too much of the 'wrong' food will ensure the cycle is repeated over and over. A lot of my clients tell me that if they eat a couple of cakes from a box, they feel the familiar feelings of guilt, they feel fat, and think 'what the hell, I may as well eat the lot'. Of course, eating the lot only serves to create stronger feelings of guilt, and so the cycle is reinforced.

When you're on a prescriptive diet that dictates what and when you can eat, your 'thinking' brain is logically following the instructions, and it feels great when the weight comes off. But what happens when you stop the diet? You look for a substitute for that feel good feeling, and the fastest route to comforting yourself is food. You start to have that little bit of extra food on your plate, or a pudding at the restaurant, and your focus of attention soon shifts back to feeling anxious as your weight increases again, and your primitive brain is back in the driving seat. The weight will inevitably creep back on when you stop a diet, because you're operating with a different part of the brain, over which you have no conscious control – the emotional limbic system.

Sugar

What food substance gives you the most pleasure for a quick fix? Sugar! Sugar stimulates the release of serotonin, a neurotransmitter that makes us feel good. Insulin stimulates the serotonin to be taken up by the brain, which in turn lifts our mood. As soon as the sugar high is reduced, so does the serotonin, and you lose that feel good factor. The feelings of anxiety about the sugar intake, together with the need for another 'fix' will send you searching for another 'high' that comes from simple carbohydrates, or sugars.

Food is a very high reward system when you're feeling anxious or stressed. The reward is both psychological and physiological, satisfying the mind and body. But the reward has a price if you're experiencing anxiety, as guilt together with weight gain can create more anxiety, low self-esteem and loss of self-confidence.

The role of hormones

When you experience chronic (long term) stress and anxiety, coupled with an intake of sugary, fatty foods, the body produces more cortisol and insulin, both of which increase your appetite. These hormones also drive you to eat more 'instant reward' foods high in sugar and fats. When you have eaten more than is needed, the storage levels of your liver reach their limit, and the excess sugar is converted into fatty acids. These fatty acids are released into your bloodstream, where they are stored as fat in the areas you least want it such as your waist, hips and bottom. Once these regions of your body have more than enough of the fat storage, the fatty acids will travel to other areas of your body such as your heart and kidneys. It is easy to see where this could lead to isn't it?

Sleep

Then there are your sleeping patterns. If you sleep well, and have a good amount of restorative sleep, your body produces leptin, a hormone which tells you when to stop eating. If your sleep is frequently disturbed, or of poor quality, your body will produce more of a hormone called ghrelin, which increases your appetite. Another cycle is created. Bad sleep-lack of energy-sugar cravings for energy-higher carbohydrate intake-lethargy and tiredness-lack of exercise-anxiety-restless sleep= WEIGHT GAIN.

Don't be fooled by 'low fat healthy' foods. The lower level of fat content is compensated for by higher levels of sugar to give the food taste, which will turn to fat in the body eventually. Fat storage has a way of acting as a comforter (i.e. no famine, preparing to survive the harshest conditions in primitive times), and so it becomes a double edged sword.

Temporary rewards

If you experience the anxiety-eat-guilt-anxiety-eat cycle you have given your brain a programme to run that brings false, temporary rewards. It is a form of self-medicating, and can also be seen as an addiction in some people. If you have uncomfortable feelings that you don't want to or can't face, then you are literally pushing them down by eating excessive amounts of food. Eating continually and excessively stops you consciously thinking about the reasons for your anxiety and stress, because you are in a constant state of being comforted. But the feelings are still there, and until you address those feelings and the reasons behind them, the cycle will continue, no matter how many diets you try. Apart from anything else, let's face it, diets are restrictive, and you will eventually feel bored by having to follow someone else's rules.

By continuing with the cycle of overeating and eating unhealthy food to comfort yourself, you are feeding the anxiety itself, as well as setting yourself up for possible future health problems. A lot of overweight clients do worry continually about their health, but as that only adds to their already anxious thought processes, it becomes another component of the ever strengthening cycle.

Later in this book I will give you some simple strategies to retrain your brain into seeing food as sustenance and not an emotional support. By reading this book you are already giving your brain a powerful message that change is about to happen. You are the only one in charge of the instructions you give to your brain. Your choices are yours, no one else's – feels good to be in control doesn't it! You're on your way to being slim and sassy!

Chapter Two

IDENTIFYING PERSONAL TRIGGERS, REWARDS AND CONSEQUENCES

Now you know how your brain creates your drivers to eat when you're feeling emotional, you are on your way to controlling those urges to eat, and using the power of your brain to your advantage. You will be able to lose weight, reduce your anxiety, and bring on the slim and sassy you!

Let's look first of all at some of the generic triggers, consequences and rewards associated with mindlessly eating to escape emotions. Hopefully you'll be able to spot your own 'push buttons' in there somewhere!

Triggers: feelings

- Feeling lonely
- Feeling tired and irritable
- Feeling angry
- Feeling stressed
- Being bored

- Feeling powerless over cravings
- Feeling helpless about situation

Triggers: situations

- Chronic pain or discomfort
- Being unhappy in relationship
- Being unfulfilled at work
- Hormonal imbalance due to excessive cortisol in bloodstream
- Peer pressure
- Poor sleep

Triggers: actions

- Self-punishment
- Guilt
- Self-loathing
- Low self esteem
- Need for reward
- Need for compensation
- Eating to avoid feeling emotions
- Habits (these can be linked to place, a time of day or a routine)

Consequences and rewards (of your actions lead)

- Temporary self-soothing (reward)
- Temporary self-medicating (reward)
- Temporary sugar high (reward)
- Distanced from real emotions (reward)
- Quietens the limbic system, so temporary reduction in negative emotions (reward)
- Anxiety-eat-guilt-anxiety cycle spirals. Long term stress

means the adrenals produce more cortisol which increases cravings for high sugar, fat and salt foods. (Consequences)

- Anxiety and stress disturb sleep, which means you produce more of the hormone Ghrelin, which drives you to eat. (Consequences)
- Insulin levels are increased with high sugar intake, creating an increased hunger. (Consequences)
- Overeating of high sugar and fat content foods can create an addiction in some people. (Consequences)
- Your brain continues to run the same programme with the same behaviour as your weight increases, and your anxiety rises. (Consequences)
- Withdrawal from others, including sexual partner. (Consequences)
- Avoidance of social situations (Consequences and Reward)
- Excessive weighing (Obsessive consequences)
- Mirror loathing (Consequences)
- Eating becomes a mindless habit rather than a pleasure (Consequential habit)
- You use clothes to hide your body (Consequential behaviour)
- The more you mindlessly eat, the more you are pushing down your emotions. (Temporary reward)

Quite a list isn't it? You may have noticed how the consequences far outstrip the rewards. Did you spot some of your own triggers in there? It could be that your trigger(s) feel like something that only you have got, but I promise you if you feel it, others will also experience similar feelings.

What can you do to break the cycle ?

When you are feeling caught in a downward spiral of anxiety and eating, it can seem as if there is no way out. It's a bit like being in a maze. You see the entrance, and make a mental note of how you got into the maze, but it can seem impossible to find a way out – and that can produce feelings of high anxiety and panic in some people.

Your personal maze

Think of your mind as your own personal maze. Ask where you were before the anxiety and overeating started – in other words, where was the beginning of your maze?

Then ask yourself the following questions:

- What were you doing that you're not doing now?
- Do you have the same people around you now?
- Were you living and working in the same place that you are now?
- Did you shop in the same way and in the same place that you do now?
- How did you see yourself then?
- What significant events happened in your life before the anxiety and overeating started?

Then there are your core beliefs. Maybe you've always been an anxious person. Perhaps you were overweight as a child. Maybe your family are overweight. Could it be that you believe you're genetically disposed to being fat?

If you've said 'yes' to any or all of the scenarios in the above paragraph, let's look at it another way.

Choice and habit

If you say you've always been an anxious person, aren't you just a little bit fed up with that anxiety by now? Don't you owe it to yourself to at least see what it feels like to be calm and in control of your choices?

It is a choice you know, and it's also a habit. If you believe you've always been anxious, you're generalising your life to include an expectation of the rest of it being anxiety filled!

What you believe, you expect, and what you expect, you get!

Were you overweight as a child? Why was that? Did your parents over-feed you? Did you live on sweets? Were meal times high-reward times? Were your parents very busy, so meal times were more like ongoing snack times? Whatever the reason, you're not a child any more. Now you have the choice to do something about it. Will you take it, or forever remain as the fat child?

Behaviour and emotion

Were your family overweight and do you believe it's all down to genetics? There is a new corner of science called epigenetics, which means our environment can trigger our genes' behaviour, or switch them off. Our environment doesn't change our DNA, just the expression of our genes. Some people do have what is known as 'Epigenetic Inheritance', meaning some of the experiences of the parents may pass to future generations, but that is more about behaviour than DNA structure, and behaviour can be changed.

Maybe, just maybe, if your family are all overweight, they overeat, or eat too much of the high sugar and fat foods? Perhaps they don't exercise very much? Asking these questions may challenge your belief that we can blame our gene pool on our behaviours and size – it isn't necessarily so.

Changing your mind

Back to you. If you feel powerless over your cravings for sweet and/or fatty foods, is it really the cravings you're powerless over? Or is it the emotions you are pushing down with all that food? By allowing yourself to acknowledge your emotions, however uncomfortable they may be, you are interrupting that programme that your brain is running. Of course, sometimes you just don't know why you feel the way you do, and that's the time to see a professional therapist.

With the help of a professional, you can be guided to uncover and face the cause of your emotions in a safe and supportive environment. Once you have cleared away the old causes, the emotions will dissolve, along with the urgent need for comfort from food.

Much of your brain has no concept of time, and when you're caught in the habitual spiral of anxiety and eating based on old memories, to your brain the events of the memories are happening now. It may have been going on for a long time, but only you know that consciously and rationally, not your pre conscious brain!

Your mind is powerful enough to create anxiety and food cravings based on something that may have happened a long time ago. This means the good news is that your mind is also powerful enough to accept and implement change now.

Personal motivation

So, what is your personal motivation to change? A lot of clients tell me they just want to be slimmer, happier, healthier, and more attractive. Having those aims is a good start, but it is in no way enough to make permanent changes, because it is too vague, and your brain needs clear instructions!

Your pre conscious thinking processes start in the primitive part of your brain, where there is no rationale or logic. By the time the thought has passed through the first two ancient parts of your brain (remember them?) the decision to do something has already been made, based on what you've done before.

When it comes into your consciousness, or thinking part of your brain, you then attach emotions to your actions, such as guilt, pleasure, regret, shame or any of the other emotions that you may feel when you've overindulged in unhealthy habits due to your emotions. The first part of your brain doesn't question anything, so you need to be very specific about what your requirements are!

Decide your requirements

Let's say you want to be slimmer. You will need to know your current weight – go on, get on the scales! It's just a number that will be changed, so at the start of your journey you simply need to write down somewhere what the scales tell you now.

The next thing to decide is what your goal weight is, and this is the tricky part, because you do need to be realistic. If anxiety is clouding your judgment, put this exercise away for another day when you know with absolute certainty that you are going to change.

Timeframe

Suppose you currently weigh 16 stone, and your goal weight is 12 stone. That would appear to be realistic, but unless you put a time frame on it, it isn't. There is no good saying: 'I want to lose four stone', because you haven't given your brain a timeframe to work with, which makes the goal as strong as fresh air!

The average weight loss, when done safely and with lifestyle changes rather than diet, is 2 lbs each week. If you say 'I want to lose an average of 8-10 lbs each month starting from the beginning of next month,' that is a specific, realistic and achievable goal, provided you make the necessary changes to achieve the weight loss.

Specific goal

Once you have decided on a time frame, a realistic weight loss goal, and can actually see yourself in your mind's eye making all the lifestyle changes needed for achievement, your brain has a very loud and clear message that change is happening!

It's a bit like a child writing out a Christmas present list to Santa. Just saying 'I would like a doll' will inevitably bring the child the wrong one!! Always be very specific about what you want and when, and then you have a clear goal to start planning how you're going to get there.

Suppose your wish is to be happier? Happiness is a very subjective emotion. What makes you happy might make the next person miserable! Again, definition is needed, and it must be realistic and achievable.

What do you think will create your increase in happiness? Is it being slimmer? Is it being healthier? Is it being in control of your choices, which can result in you being slimmer and healthier?

Could it be wearing a certain outfit, and seeing admiring glances from others. Identifying your specific target for increased happiness is just as important as knowing what your goal weight is.

All of your emotions are interlinked, so by addressing one area of concern, it usually follows that other areas fall into a better place. When you identify your true goals in this way, you are really getting to know yourself, rather than just skimming the surface of who you are.

Being healthier is an easier goal, as just by losing the excess weight you are increasing your chances of a healthier body and mind. Being overweight brings a whole list of potential health issues, not least of all joint pain, high blood pressure, diabetes and a strain on your heart, so it stands to reason that losing weight will reduce those risks.

The point of choice

You were not born to be fat! You have a choice (medical conditions aside). You can stay fat, miserable and wrap yourself in self-pity and anxiety, or you can get up and do something about it! I'm guessing you are going to use that powerful mind of yours and become the person you were meant to be, otherwise you would be reading *Burgers Weekly* instead of this book.

Identifying where your personal cycle starts is a powerful way to push the stop button. It's the chicken and egg question – what comes first for you – anxiety or eating? Do you eat because you're anxious, or are you anxious because you overeat? Although it does end up as a cycle of repeated behaviour and emotions, finding the first part of your own maze will lead to the escape route from your current way of being.

Making change is a value game. If the benefits of losing weight outweigh (no pun intended) the cost for you, you're on your way.

What will you choose? Fat or Slim? Frumpy or Sassy? In control of food, or will food continue to control you?

Your choice – you already know the answer!

Here's to being Slim and Sassy!

Chapter Three

ARE YOU HEAD HUNGRY OR STOMACH HUNGRY?

'STRESSED' SPELLED BACKWARDS = DESSERTS!!

That statement could be called the definition of head hungry! When you're stressed or anxious sweet foods are the fastest way to fire up your brain's reward centres.

A lot of people believe that you eat with your eyes, but when it comes to stress and anxiety, you eat with your emotions without logical thought or planning. Knowing the difference, and identifying your own triggers to eat is the key to successful weight loss, so relax and get ready to know yourself even better!

So what does head hungry mean, exactly?

It means your desire for food is not physical, it's psychological. You could have just eaten a large meal and be very full, but that little corner of anxiety or stress in your mind tells you that you want some form of reward.

Remember childhood bribes? "If you eat all your dinner

you can have some sweets?". It's no coincidence that you might crave a sweet dessert after a heavy meal if subconsciously you feel there is something 'missing' from your life, or you're feeling stressed because deep down it can remind you of childhood and comfort.

When you are eating with your emotions, the pleasure of mindlessly eating something with a very desirable taste temporarily masks your emotions. It is a few moments of pleasure that takes your mind to a different place as your brain releases dopamine. Dopamine makes you feel good. It is a neurotransmitter that plays a key role in how you respond to pleasure. When the dopamine is released and the good feelings follow, the reward centre that has fired up in your brain will remember the pleasure of the reward, and seek to repeat the pleasure more and more. You learn to respond to pleasure, and as we're talking about the reward of food here, that cycle of learned response and expectation can create not only cravings but addiction to certain foods, mainly those containing sugar. (We will be looking at sugar in greater detail in the next chapter).

Dopamine creates the *desire* for the pleasure, not the pleasure itself, so even if you think about a piece of chocolate cake, the same brain process is fired up, as if you had actually eaten the cake.

When you overeat, or nibble constantly at sugary snacks, you're keeping your dopamine levels high, and therefore the reward system in your brain is switched on all the time. If you have low levels of dopamine, you are more likely to overeat unhealthy foods to fire up that feeling of pleasurable satisfaction. It doesn't stop at just sweet foods, although those are the most rewarding, greasy, fatty foods often feature too.

When you are young, if mealtimes were a happy time and the time when you had attention if, as an adult you are lonely, you are more likely to subconsciously attempt to recreate that feeling with food. As I said, it isn't always sweet foods that people crave, sometimes it's a Big Mac and fries!

This is because unfortunately, unhealthy foods trigger the brain's reward system faster than healthy foods. As sweet and fatty foods are calorie dense, more dopamine is released as it is calorie responsive. The more dopamine your brain produces, the better you feel!

Over time, the more unhealthy the diet, the higher the reward, and the more desensitised the dopamine becomes. This means you will eat more to get more!

Dopamine and mind power

You can see why the restriction of diets can result in cravings once the diet stops! If you're short of dopamine, your brain will drive you to get some!

When you use the power of your mind to retrain your dopamine response and reward centres to respond in the same way to healthy food, weight loss becomes easy and permanent.

Not that easy to do, I hear you say! Not so easy on your own I agree, unless you have immense will power, but then you are setting yourself up subconsciously to object to the changes. With the help of hypnotherapy you can completely change your mindset, and take back control. Once you have retrained your brain to fire up the dopamine for healthy food, you're on your way to a much calmer, healthier way of living. It can be done, and believe me once you have let your brain know that healthy food is good, your energy levels will soar, your skin will glow, you will sleep better, you will say goodbye to generalised anxiety, and find that irritability and irrational cravings are a thing of the past.

When you've got your brain on the right track and eating small, regular healthy meals with healthy snacks between if needed, your reward system stays switched on, but for the right reasons. You can keep your dopamine levels topped up by making sure you include vitamin B6 and Vitamin E in your diet. Dark fruits such as berries will provide the antioxidants, keeping your dopamine neurons healthy and happy.

If you are someone who craves sweet and unhealthy foods, it's important for you to recognise your personal triggers. It could be a daily activity, such as the sweet trolley at work, or walking by a cake shop, the smell of burgers and chips (yes, even that can seem appealing when you're needing that dopamine fix!), or even a certain emotion.

If you know you have addictive cravings to certain foods, over time it can lead to more anxiety and stress as you might try to hide the addictive behaviour from those around you. I often see clients who eat in their car, in the bathroom, or in the middle of the night when everyone else is asleep. The clients who eat in secret like this are also feeding their anxiety and stress, as guilt and shame are very powerful emotions.

So many people think they are weak if they have any form of addiction, but that isn't the case. It's the need for higher dopamine levels that drive the behaviour, and when you know that, you can let go of the guilt and hold your head high as you take back control.

Naturally create dopamine

There are foods that naturally create the release of dopamine. As your body needs amino acids to create dopamine, lean meat is one choice. Proteins from lean meat contain all the essential amino acids that your body is unable to produce on its own. Fruits, vegetables, cheese, yogurts, nuts and seeds also stimulate the release of dopamine, so once you've said goodbye to the sugary and fatty foods, you will still feel good from the dopamine – it's a brain retrain! (By the way, a small amount of dark chocolate is a good source of the precursors to dopamine, but remember the word small!).

So to give an overview of head hungry, here's a few

indicators that your eating habits are emotion based, not hunger based:

- Cravings are instant and call for instant gratification – there's no thought attached.
- If you binge eat, or eat the whole bar or packet of something unhealthy, you're head hungry.
- Happiness and celebration can trigger head hunger – it's all emotions, whether negative or positive.
- Your cravings are for sweet, salty or fatty foods.
- You eat a lot of carbohydrates for comfort.
- You can't remember what you ate yesterday.
- You eat so fast you don't even taste the food a lot of the time.
- You feel guilty or ashamed after you've eaten.
- You have single track focus – think about the food or see it, want it, eat it.
- The craving or desire is intense and nothing will stop it until you eat.
- You link foods to habitual behaviour, such as watching a programme on TV, sitting in a certain chair or at a certain time.
- You're tired and can't be bothered to cook.
- You have low self-esteem, and feel like food controls your life.
- You feel helpless about your choices of what you eat.

Some steps you can take to STOP the cycle:

Keep a food and emotion journal. Each time you reach for unhealthy food due to a craving, take a moment to write down how you're feeling and what the food is doing for you. If you do this before you actually put the food into your mouth, you may well find you don't eat it anyway, because you've fired up a different part of your brain. Also write down how you feel afterwards if you do eat. Be honest, you're on a new road and moving away from old behaviours.

Deal with your emotions and triggers. Don't bottle your emotions up, talk to someone, whether it's a professional or someone close to you.

Remove all temptation from your home, car and workplace. If it's not there, you can't eat it, and the craving WILL pass.

Physically get up and move. Go for a walk, run a bath, play with the dog or dance around the garden – whatever works for you. It stops the cravings.

Do something else. Once you've eaten, get up and do something else that's not related to food.

Take a 'fat photo' of yourself and keep it on your phone. Look at it constantly to remind yourself that you are beautiful underneath those layers, and you are working towards revealing that slim and sassy you. If you have a photo of when you were slimmer, put that on your 'phone too – make it a goal to update that photo to the very near future.

Feel gorgeous every day! Wear perfume, put on make-up every day, even if you're not going out. You're too beautiful to hide away! Feel good about yourself – you weren't born to be fat!

Act as if you are that slim, gorgeous woman at all times. Pay attention to your posture, and walk tall with your head high. Smile at others, smile at your own reflection, and most of all, tell yourself every day that you are beautiful and way too fit to be fat!

Have a realistic weight goal. Know that every day you are moving closer to it.

Buy an outfit that will fit you at your realistic goal weight. Hang it up in your bedroom on the outside the wardrobe, and know you will be wearing it in the not-too-distant future.

Give yourself ten minutes. If the cravings happen, give yourself ten minutes. Time it, drink some water while you're waiting and move to a different place. Usually the cravings will float away.

Relax. If you're bored, see it as a chance to relax. Some people crave time to themselves, it's a luxury. If you're someone who finds it hard to relax, see being bored as an opportunity to do something you've been putting off (like sorting out those old 'fat' clothes that are not connected to the new you).

Get enough sleep. Reading before you sleep is a great way to tire your eyes, and it feels great when you can close them and drift off.

Avoid watching TV or using the laptop or tablet at bedtime. It will stimulate your brain, which could lead to thoughts of food.

Always remember that you own your choices. You are the only person who is responsible for what you eat, so you can choose to choose what's good for you.

Food that nurtures your body will nurture your soul.

How do you recognise if you are stomach hungry?

- It is some time since you last ate – at least 3-4 hours.
- Your stomach is growling.
- The hunger comes on gradually, and increases slowly.
- You feel shaky.
- You can't focus mentally.
- You feel tired because your body needs fuel for energy.
- Healthy food is appetising.
- You take time to think about what you'd like to eat.
- You imagine the food once you've decided what you'd like.
- You don't feel emotional – just hungry.
- You look forward to eating the food.
- You eat slowly and mindfully, really tasting and appreciating the food.
- You feel comfortably full.
- You feel energised after eating, with a clearer mind.

- You don't feel shame or guilt after eating.

Score your hunger level, with 1 being starving, and 10 being full. You're stomach hungry if it's around 5.

Drink a glass of water, and if you're still hungry ten minutes later, you need to eat.

You notice that the first mouthful tastes the best.

Final thoughts

When did you last eat? If it's only 1-2 hours ago it's probably head hunger. (A breakfast with protein is far better for weight control than skipping breakfast.)

Make sure you eat some healthy food every three hours to maintain your blood sugar levels and reduce the chance of craving unhealthy food.

Slice up a lemon and always have ice cubes in the freezer for a refreshing glass of iced lemon water which you can sip throughout the day.

Have some healthy snacks in the fridge, such as veggie and fruit sticks (carrots, celery, apple, pineapple, cucumber), and have a nibble when you feel the need.

Put stickers on your fridge, cupboards and mirrors saying 'Fat Off to being a fatty!' 'I'm way too fit to be fat!'

What are you feeling before and after you eat? Does your mood change for the better after you've eaten?

What is the food doing for you? Is it nourishing your body or feeding your emotions?

Why do you overeat?

What or who is the strongest influence on your anxiety levels and food choices?

If you weren't eating what would you be doing?

Are you moving forward towards being slimmer and healthier, or are you standing still, or even taking a step or two backwards?

Are you connecting food to other habits, such as always sitting in the same chair in front of the TV while you eat?

Are your energy levels fluctuating constantly?

What will change about you when you're slimmer and calmer?

How will those close to you react to the new slimmer, happier you?

Will being slimmer result in you doing something that you're currently avoiding? (Be very honest with yourself when answering this question, because it might be something you need to sort out before you can achieve successful, permanent weight loss).

What opportunities will you have when you're slim and healthy that you don't have now as a fat person?

You might find a few more questions to ask yourself. So long as you make sure you answer your own questions with absolute honesty you can move forward to being the slim and sassy woman you deserve to be!

Having a very clear and honest insight into who you are, and why you overeat or reach for unhealthy, fattening foods gives you power – use that power to take back control and make the changes to melt the fat – no more excuses!

Here's to being Slim and Sassy!

Chapter Four

SUGAR – YOU'RE SWEETER WITHOUT IT!

It has long been a myth that fat is the main enemy of successful weight loss, but it's sugar that anxiety craves, and sugar that can pile on the weight.

Little wonder that those 'low fat healthy' snacks don't produce weight loss and satisfaction in the long term. The taste and reward has to come from somewhere, otherwise the products would never be bought by unsuspecting dieters. Low fat usually means high sugar!

In the previous chapter we looked at the reward system in the brain, and how sugar sends that reward system into orbit, creating dopamine-driven cravings. The reward from sugar can be as strong as the reward from drugs to sugar-sensitive individuals.

It's the reason children want more and more sweets once they've had the taste. The feelings from a sugary snack can be immensely pleasurable, but equally strong can be the guilty aftermath if increased weight and self-loathing are the result.

Don't panic, I'm not going to suggest here that you start living on lettuce leaves, but knowledge is power, and power can mean successful weight loss through a healthy mindset. So, let's have a look at that innocent little spoonful of sugar shall we?

Whether you take sugar in your tea, or sprinkle it on your breakfast, that sugar is just the tip of the iceberg. The hidden sugars in processed and refined foods amount to an alarming daily intake for those on a less than healthy diet.

There is a big difference between naturally occurring sugars in fruit and vegetables and the added sugars that manufacturers use to appeal to your taste buds. You need some carbohydrates for energy. Excessive sugar intake is not only a sure way to gain and maintain weight, but it's also a potential road to many diseases, such as Type 2 Diabetes and fatty liver diseases. As I've mentioned before, sugar stimulates the same reward areas of the brain as strong drugs, and can be just as addictive in some individuals. Sugar can be so addictive to some people that in the 18th century it was carried in small pouches and used much like snuff to give a little lift.

What sugar does to you

Let's look at the following effects of a high sugar intake perhaps some of it may come as a surprise!

- Sugar can add weight around the waist if excessive amounts are being stored as fat. Waist fat is known as visceral fat. Visceral fat is linked to heart disease.
- The liver stores excess sugar as fat, raising triglycerides, which can cause a fatty liver.
- Cholesterol mixes with triglycerides, forming a dense low density lipoprotein, which can block arteries.
- Too much sugar in the bloodstream triggers the pancreas

to release insulin. Insulin tells the cells to take up the glucose from the bloodstream and use it for energy. The more sugar you eat, the more insulin is released as the body desperately tries to use the excess glucose. Glucose not used for energy is stored as fat.

- If blood sugar falls too low, glycogen is released by the liver (glycogen is your reserve glucose store). Once that's been used, your body will send out distress signals and adrenaline is released into the bloodstream.
- Adrenaline can feed anxiety as the physical response to it can include shakiness and light-headedness. You feel tired from adrenal fatigue, and need a quick energy boost. What do you subconsciously reach for? Yes, you've got it, something sweet with a fast reward hit to your brain! This isn't true for every person of course, but if you're sugar sensitive (and we'll check that out in a moment or two), your response will be that much more noticeable.
- Some juices such as apple and cranberry contain more sugar than coke!
- Look out for hidden sugars in pasta sauces, table sauces, pickles and low fat dressings.
- If packaging has a picture of the countryside, sunshine or other nature pictures, check the sugar content!

Hidden sugars same problems

Table sugar is 50 percent sucrose and 50 fructose(fruit sugar). It's the fructose that gives you the highest reward, because it's higher than sugar on the sweetness scale.

If packaged food lists sugar in the first three ingredients, step away if you want healthy weight loss!

Remember that simple carbohydrates (refined, processed foods, white bread and pasta, white rice, cakes, biscuits etc) are more readily available as glucose within your body. As they give a short term energy lift almost immediately, there will follow an energy crash, where your brain will drive you to seek more quick energy giving food.

Eating complex carbohydrates such as brown rice, wholemeal bread and pasta, potatoes in their skins, lentils, beans, vegetables and fruit will sustain you for much longer because they are slowly released. There is no sudden rush upwards, so no sudden crash downwards!

Let's have a look at why some sugars (and sweeteners) are so appealing because of their sweetness. Just a few variations of sugars found in common everyday food, with the sweetness rating.

Natural sweetener Stevia	300
Fructose	1.4
Sucrose	1.0
Corn syrup	1.0
Glucose	0.7
Maltose (found in beer)	0.3
Lactose (found in milk)	0.2

In an individual who is sugar sensitive, the extreme highs and lows of their blood sugar can play havoc with their weight and their moods.

Signs that you may be sugar sensitive:

1.Sometimes you feel absolutely full of energy, and feel you can do anything and everything that needs doing.

2.You suddenly feel absolutely drained after the initial rush of energy. You can't think straight, your motivation is lost, and you just want to sleep.

3.You have a lot of headaches during the ups and downs of your energy highs and lows.

4.You feel irritable or angry for no apparent reason.

5.You see the negatives all around you.

6.You don't like yourself much but don't really know why.
7.No matter what diets you try, you soon give up and the weight just sits there, covering up the real slim and sassy you.
8.Your sex drive has taken a holiday.
9.You use every excuse to avoid exercise because you just can't be bothered.
10.You skip breakfast because it's too much effort, you haven't got time, the cat drank the milk, or your fridge has been burgled.
11.Your sleep is disturbed, and you wake up tired, feeling as if you have been dreaming all night.
12.If you see, smell, or think about sweet treats, you feel absolutely compelled to eat them, and you don't stop at one.
13.You feel like a failure because you can't lose weight.
14.You feel like food controls you.
15.Sometimes you feel shaky and have palpitations. (This is because your blood sugar glucose is all over the place, but is often mistaken for a panic attack).
16.Your mood is mostly low and/or you are being treated for depression.
17.You have asked your GP to change your medication more than once because it didn't seem to be working.
18.You feel out of balance with yourself.
19.You crave carbohydrates, sometimes you even buy sweets pretending they are for the kids!
20.When you eat carbs you feel (temporarily) good about yourself (as your self-esteem is raised short-term).

Calories are irrelevant if you're sugar sensitive. 1 gram of fat equates to 9 calories, while 1 gram of sugar equals only 4 calories. *It's how those calories are used that's important in sugar-sensitive individuals*. You can eat a 'low fat, low calorie' meal and be filling yourself up with sugars that will play havoc with your energy levels and your mood!

Even if you're not sugar sensitive, cutting right down on

your intake by being aware of hidden sugars will go a very long way towards healthy weight loss.

Some sneaky labelling – these are all sugars

Sucrose
Glucose
Honey
Corn syrup
Invert sugar
Fructose
Molasses
Maltose
Hydrolysed starch
Cane sugar
Brown sugar
Fructose corn syrup
Fruit juice concentrate
Crystalline sucrose

The higher up the list of ingredients, the more of it there is.

Decoding the labels

Make it your business to see past the disguise!

4 grams = 1 teaspoon

Women should aim for no more than 30 grams per day, which equates to 7.5 teaspoons.

On labels, where the words 'Carbohydrates (of which sugars)' is shown, be aware that more than 22.5g per 100g is a high level of sugars, while 5g or less is low.

Foods labels that state 'no added sugar' means that no additional sugar has been added. It doesn't mean it's sugar free, just that the sugars contained in the product are from a natural source.

In order to be slim and sassy (in other words, gorgeous with bags of self-confidence – the you inside that wants to come out to play!), you have to also be savvy when it comes to shopping. It will take a while longer at first until you get used to reading labels, but believe me, once you've mastered the art, you'll find yourself avoiding the sweet stuff without thinking about it.

Because sugar has such a high comfort factor, it is all too easy to say 'well, I'll just eat this giant-sized cake today but then I'll be good for the rest of the week'. That's great if you can stick to it. Eating sensibly and healthily 80 percent of the time, and having a little of what you fancy 20 percent of the time is an enjoyable way to melt the fat and raise your self-esteem and confidence, because as soon as you can reconcile the fact that it is only you who is in control of what you eat and how much you exercise, the sooner you'll be slim, sassy and proud of it!

Diets don't give you that choice, because they're prescriptive and you don't really have to put in much effort so long as you follow the instructions. When you really take control and change your mindset to that of someone who chooses to eat healthy food because she wants to look and feel good, the change becomes permanent. You don't have someone else spelling it all out for you. You have to be aware and be mindful of how you shop and what you eat. That means being mindful of yourself, and welcoming every change you make towards revealing that slim and sassy you.

The importance of exercise

You now know about your brain, your body and what it does with the food you eat, but how do you utilise the energy that good food gives you? Have you ever watched someone who really enjoys exercise? They tend to smile a lot, have sparkling eyes and clear skin, not to mention a good body shape.

You'll remember (I hope!) that if you are a sugar-sensitive person you probably can't be bothered to exercise due to the ever changing highs and lows of your energy levels. You might feel like running for ever during the short-term highs, but as soon as the crash comes you just want to flop somewhere and eat. Even if you're not sugar sensitive, you may not have found a form of exercise that you like. Perhaps you see it as something you 'should' do, and therefore rebel against it subconsciously? Perhaps you are one of the people who make endless excuses not to move that body into better shape?

Not conducive to being slim and sassy at all is it?

I'm not a great one for going to the gym. I've tried it and got bored, because like a diet, I felt I was being told what to do (bit of a rebel inside!). I felt that everyone else in the gym had better bodies, so I let the membership lapse.

What you enjoy

I'm very aware of the importance of exercise, but I am someone who needs to make her own choices, so I set about looking for some form of exercise that I could really enjoy and would do every day, because I looked forward to it.

Extreme ballet was out, as was mountaineering, so I settled on walking the dog. Not just a quick nip around the block, but two walks each day of around 45 minutes to 1 hour each. I probably look a bit odd to other dog walkers who seem to stroll lazily around the fields where I live, because I actually go on what my husband calls a route march! If I'm going to walk, I want my body to work for me, so no matter what the weather the dog gets dragged out (she doesn't seem to mind) with me. Both of us are a lot fitter because of it, and my slim and sassy mindset (and the dog's) is definitely in charge.

Whatever you do, whether it's going to the gym, swimming, walking, jazzercise, dancercise, bouncing around on a trampoline or running up and down stairs, make sure it's something you know you look forward to, and never accept your own excuses not to do it! If you do start making excuses or missing the odd day, ask yourself if you need to change to a different form of exercise. Make exercise a part of your everyday fight against fat and you will be heading for slim, gorgeous and healthy!

It goes without saying that if you have any form of medical condition you must speak to your GP before embarking on any form of exercise.

Here's to being Slim and Sassy!

Chapter Five

MY PERSONAL STORY

I want to share with you the personal experiences that have formed part of the reason I wrote this book. I hope it will help you.

Although I have never been very fat, I have certainly been heavier than I needed to be, and have also experienced the effect unresolved emotions can have on my relationship with food.

When I was in my early teens, I experienced an action by a male family member that my young mind couldn't cope with at the time. I won't go into details, but I'm sure you can work it out!

My first response was to tell my mother what had happened, as she was my immediate source of comfort. Don't get me wrong, my mother was a very caring and supportive person generally, but her response to this particular incident was to tell me to forget it and put it down to 'just one of those things'. Don't talk, don't tell, just forget. To make matters worse, the same family member committed a similar offence against another young girl a few months later, and when that went to court, my parents gave him an excellent character reference! By that time feelings of not being valued were deeply embedded in my subconscious.

Strange behaviour around food

So life carried on. 'The Incident' was never mentioned, and no one ever asked me if I was okay. Unaware at the time of what was going on inside my own subconscious (I didn't even know what the subconscious *was* at that time), I eventually found myself beginning to behave in a very strange way around food. Looking back it really was quite bizarre, and although I understand now as a professional therapist, my dear mum was seemingly oblivious.

It started off with bread rolls and tomatoes. Looking back it was the start of a form of bulimia, but at the time I would only eat endless bread rolls and tomatoes. Rather than rocking the boat my mum simply went out and bought more bread and more tomatoes each day. Talking about my strange behaviour was never mentioned during the silent delivery of yet another pile of the unusual diet contents.

After a while another strange thing happened. The tomatoes took on a dreadful smell; although I still ate them because they tasted nice I would hold my nose and munch away, while my mum would constantly sniff at the fruit telling me the smell was all in my mind (which of course it was!).

I would eat as many bread rolls and tomatoes as I could possibly fit in, then make myself sick. The relief on vomiting was liberating. My young mind had some form of control in getting out that which had gone in (both physically and psychologically), and so it carried on for some time. Again, it was a case of don't talk, don't tell, just forget, or in my mum's case, ignore it and it will go away!

Nobody ever mentioned my strange behaviour, so inadvertently the feeling of not being important was reinforced and magnified in my mind.

After a while I moved on to grapefruits (cleansing effect). The tomato smell had finally got too much for me, and grapefruit just seemed so much nicer. I'm sure you're getting the picture by now! Of course, the supply of grapefruits was never ending (very healthy if nothing else!), and eventually I slid into a full-blown breakdown which ensured a sharp exit from school (I didn't mind as I was literally away with the fairies). Still no one mentioned or acknowledged the original incident.

Throughout the following years my mind's need to control worked its way through overeating, undereating, marrying someone very controlling (vicarious control?), and by the time I was just 19, subsequent divorce and an excruciating custody battle for my beautiful daughter. I now know that all of this was a desperate need for control and recognition. I hadn't been listened to, so food became a great source of comfort (if not nutrition!).

Don't talk, don't tell, just forget.

Hiding feelings

I thought I was being very strong when it came to dealing with emotions, always hiding my feelings behind a wall of eating, drinking and rebellious behaviour. No one ever knew how I felt inside, and I made sure they never found out. I was ashamed of what had happened at the age of 13, even though of course it hadn't been my fault.

When I married again it was to a man who had a free spirit, and he gave me the freedom in my own mind to be myself, to recognise and acknowledge what I'd been through, and to like myself again. Food still played a big part though, but in a completely different way.

When I met my lovely free-spirited soul mate I was literally slim and sassy. I was young and had attitude, and he taught me to channel that attitude into respecting myself more than I'd ever been able to do. I became very comfortable, safe and happy. We laughed a lot, life was carefree, and nothing mattered, including taking care of my body!

I still hadn't really dealt with the deep emotions surrounding the incident when I was 13, or the massively distressing divorce and custody fight. Just like gloss paint I put a shine on my life as if everything was hunky dory.

We lived near to a takeaway, and it soon became a habit to have at least two takeaways a week.

At weekends we would go into town and I would always eat sandwiches (white bread back then) and cakes. I had biscuits for breakfast, carbs for lunch, pies, pasties, sausages and takeaways for dinner, and cakes and sweets as treats. Exercise was a foreign word to me.

I was so happy I forgot to look in the mirror!

I was in a changing room on the day that my nutritional life changed. Getting ready for a holiday I was trying on a gorgeous bikini, which looked pretty good to my young and sassy mind. Until I saw the rear view in the mirror. What I saw absolutely shocked me into a very loud wake up call. My rear end had dropped down to have a chat with my knees, the skin on my backside and thighs looked like it was made of sponge, and I had what could only be described as some sort of built in bum bag hanging off my waist. My mind hadn't allowed me to see any of this before that moment.

I remember crying, then standing up really straight and saying (out loud) 'right, that's it, I'm not having this! I'm slim, I'm sexy, and I will not be a fat person! This stops now'.

To this day I'm not sure where it came from – maybe unspent anger about my young life experiences – but I found a resolve at that moment that I knew I could use to change aspects of my life that I could change.

And I did. The takeaways stopped, as did the biscuits, cakes, stodgy dinners and the fizzy drinks and crisps. I made it my business to learn about healthy eating; because there was no way on this planet I was going to wear the 'fat' label. My then husband (we are now divorced but great friends) wasn't going to change as he never put on an ounce. I didn't push, but I was on a mission to get back to being slim and sassy. I wanted to find me again in so many ways. The feeling of recognising that I had complete control over my own choices was like being set free from a gilded cage that I didn't know I was in.

Looks and good health

Back then it was all about how I looked, and that was my strong motivation, but now I'm older it's about good health as well. My blood pressure back then was through the roof (not surprising), and I was incredibly tired a lot of the time. I suffered from the most debilitating monthly migraines, which would mean going to bed for a couple of days at a time, and planning my whole life around them. Now my daughter has migraines, but she has the knowledge to make connections with what she eats and drinks, and has more control over hers than I ever did with mine.

Looking back, I was also quite moody, but without the knowledge I now have I was oblivious to the fact that food was playing a huge part in how I looked and felt about myself.

It took a while, and I didn't have the luxury of someone guiding me, but I lost most of the cellulite (I kept some for old times' sake), the wobbly thighs and built in bum bag were gone, and all of that happened because my personal motivation was to look good. Shallow yes, but also a very strong driver for a young woman to lose the weight and get her act together!

All eating patterns are habits, and the old habits I had so comfortably moved into were giving me such a high reward hit in my brain that I simply wanted more of the same. At no time before the mirror incident did I make any connection between what I was eating and how I looked or felt.

My habits since then have been very different.
During one very low period in my life just after my mum died and I had another divorce under my belt, I still ate very healthily but took to drinking wine with every meal, and then some.

My sugar cravings were re-emerging for comfort, and as I had control over the food intake, wine seemed like an innocent pleasure. It helped me to relax, and I enjoyed it. The problem was, I was drinking well over half a bottle every night, and of course the inevitable started to happen. The pounds were creeping back. I have never drank red wine which has the lowest sugar content, but I drank white wine which has about half a teaspoon (2 gm) of sugar in a 175ml glass.

At the time, I didn't realise that I may as well have been eating a burger with chips each day, or a large cake, as the amount of sugar intake would have been around the same.

It was only when I sat down and worked out just how much sugar I was ingesting that I could find the motivation to cut right back. There was no way I was going back to wobbly, ugly thighs and a feeling that I was getting fat! I still enjoy a small glass of wine when I'm cooking. I love Prosecco and it's my weekend treat with only 0.5 teaspoon of sugar in a flute glass.

Giving my husband the message
I met my (now) husband four years ago, and when I first saw the contents of his fridge and freezer I knew I was on a mission! Burgers, oven chips, pies, pasties, full fat cheese, biscuits, crisps and packets of cakes covered every shelf, not

to mention white bread! Now, it's not easy when you first meet someone to just wade in and tell them you're going to help them eat healthily and lose the excess weight (he was a bit of a beach ball back then), but I thought if he respected himself he just might listen. It wasn't easy, as he was convinced that healthy eating was for other people, and his diet was OK. I persevered and he reluctantly made a few small changes, although not enough to make a significant difference.

On top of his far from healthy diet, my husband is a real stress magnet, and was harbouring major resentment about his previous divorce, together with working long hours at a physically demanding job.

Two years into our relationship he suffered a major heart attack, and had to have an emergency triple by-pass. How he survived that I'll never know, but his diet has certainly changed since then without argument! He's completely changed his approach to food and drink, and the beach ball look has disappeared along with the clogged arteries. His motivation was of course probably the strongest it could be – his life!

Motivation drives you forward

Motivation plays a huge part in successfully losing weight and being slim and sassy, and once you've found yours, you'll never let it go because it will drive you forward to the shape and size you want to be!

The current suggestion from the WHO (World Health Organisation) is that we cut our daily recommended intake of sugar to six teaspoons, or 24 gm. The rates of obesity are absolutely frightening for the next generation!

At the time of writing this book, Britain's chief medical offer, Dame Sally Davies is calling for manufacturers to reduce the amount of added sugar in food and drink, and she has gone as far as recommending a sugar tax. Dame Sally has also expressed concern about alcohol consumption and its direct link to many life threatening diseases.

I learned a very valuable lesson when I changed my food and drink habits. If you ignore it, it won't go away! "Don't talk, Don't tell, Just forget" has gone. It is now "Discuss, Inform and Remember!

I'm not a lettuce crunching angel by any means, but by sticking to the 80 percent healthy and 20 percent a little of what I fancy mantra, I've maintained a healthy weight which hasn't changed with the years.

You can do the same! If something or someone has caused you upset in your past (or even currently), make sure you deal with it, or it could keep you chained to being a fatty, or at best someone who uses food to push down emotions.

Here's to being Slim and Sassy!

Chapter Six

MEET THE SUCCESSES!

The following are just some success stories of real clients, reproduced with their kind permission. The names have been changed of course to protect their right to confidentiality. Each one of these clients has gone from feeling fat and/or under confident to being slim, confident and radiant, just as you can!

Sonia's story

Sonia had initially come to me because she wanted to lose weight in time for an upcoming wedding. She had been divorced for ten years, and lived alone with her dog. She had two sons, but didn't see much of them. Sonia had a part-time job in a busy office where cakes and biscuits were a part of the working day.

Sonia had tried every diet under the sun, and had lost weight each time while on the diet, but it all came back with some extra once she'd stopped (sound familiar?) It took about five minutes of gentle questioning about how she felt regarding her divorce and current single status to reveal the real reason behind the weight gain. Sonia was lonely, and was using food as not only a comforter but as her friend, company and compensation for not having anyone in her life.

Sonia knew all about healthy eating, but had always relied on someone else, such as a diet provider or company, to relieve her of any responsibility. Once the diet stopped, Sonia was suddenly faced with having to own the responsibility of her food choices, and with no one to support her, she felt it was too much.

She felt that at 52, no one would want her, so she may as well be fat as she felt unattractive anyway. By the time she came to me, Sonia had all but written herself off. Hypnotherapy was the last resort!

Once Sonia realised her triggers, her body language changed. She had a more upright, confident position as she embraced her own power to make the right choices to lose weight.

I've seen clients change very quickly, but I think Sonia's change was the most amazing and rapid I had seen up to that point! She left my office with her head held high and a very determined stride!

During the following five sessions we followed the 'Weight off Your Plate' in-house programme, with Sonia texting me daily updates.

By the sixth session Sonia had lost over 20lbs, and was looking and feeling like a completely different person.

Sonia had found her personal motivation, which was to like and respect herself in order to make space in her heart for someone to share her life with. She had learned to say 'NO' to the office cakes and biscuits and felt good about it saying the word. She bought herself some new clothes and joined a dating site with a view to getting out and about and making new friends, and perhaps even meeting that special someone!

Anna's Story

Anna didn't consult me for weight loss initially. She felt she was out of control of her life, drinking too much, and (in her words) dating all the wrong men.

Anna was very confused about what she actually wanted from therapy at first. She was an attractive woman in her late forties, divorced, with a good job in London and quite hyper! Anna wasn't fat as such, but she said her weight was a bit more than she'd like it to be.

We worked at prioritising the things Anna wanted to change. She seemed to be racing through life, eating and drinking out most evenings and every weekend, and not getting very much sleep in between her busy work and social life.

On further discussion, Anna said that sometimes she felt as if she were on a rocket firing off into space with no control over where she was going. I asked her what would change first once she had a sense of control over her actions. To my surprise she said she wanted to learn to cook healthy food, to cut back on drinking and to have at least three nights a week where she could just go home from work and have some time to herself. Anna showed me pictures of her state-of the-art kitchen, and we agreed it would be fun to cook with all those gadgets to hand!

During subsequent sessions Anna and I talked about what she would be cooking. We talked about healthy foods that Anna could put together to make really tasty meals. Then we did some hypnosis to suggest that one small glass of wine with her meal would be something to look forward to on a couple of evenings, and iced water with lemon would be great at other times. Anna was really excited about having some time to herself, and felt she was giving herself permission to step off the merry-go-round that had been her previous life. Eating out on different dates was fun, but Anna agreed that cooking for herself and using her creative flair would give her a sense of calm control over her life.

During our final session, Anna said she felt calmer about her life for the first time in years. She had bought a few cookery books (healthy eating of course), and had even enrolled on a Japanese cookery course. She still had a happy social life, but her drinking had been cut back to a very safe limit, and she was very mindful about the foods she chose to eat in restaurants. Anna looked amazing, and said she had actually lost just under a stone in weight, which was a bonus! Her new regime of three evenings a week at home had enabled her to slow down and take stock. When we last spoke she was dating someone who she really liked, and had asked him round for dinner. Her final words when she left my office were 'watch this space'.

Tania's story

Tania's story was a happy, bubbly married woman in her late thirties. She had two children, one of two and a baby of six months. Tania said she hadn't been able to lose the 'baby weight' from her first child, and had put on more weight since having her recent baby. On asking her about her lifestyle, Tania told me she was so busy she didn't have time to eat during the day so she just ate 'healthy snack bars' and chocolate and sweets to keep her energy up. Evening meals were a bit of a hit and miss affair, since her husband worked late most evenings, and by the time she had sorted the children out, it was far easier to just 'shove something in the oven' than prepare a meal from scratch. As she ate late with her husband, it was a case of clearing away then falling asleep on the settee. Her nights were disturbed by the children, and she felt exhausted, mentally and physically. As she was talking to me she was very close to tears.

There were a lot of contributory factors to Tania's weight gain. Yes, she had put weight on during her pregnancies, but she was now ingesting a huge amount of sugar every day from the so called healthy snack bars (packed with sugar!) and other sweet stuff. The high sugar intake meant her blood sugar was spiking and crashing, and as she was taking in very few nutrients, her body and mind were using energy supplies from the reserves in the liver! Eating ready meals in a rushed way in the evenings added further to her body's distress, as did the poor quality of sleep which ensured she produced more of the hormone Ghrelin, which increases hunger.

Tania and I discussed the need for structure in her daily life around her eating. Once Tania had used the food and drink log I had given her to fill in each day, she agreed that urgent change was needed, not only for weight loss, but also for her energy levels and overall wellbeing.

We started by working through the weekly shopping list, crossing off the usual sweets, chocolate and healthy snack bars, and replacing them with fruit, nuts and seeds. I gave Tania some recipes for very simple soup which takes minutes to make and can last for two days' lunch, together with suggestions for a nutritious enjoyable snack of celery, pine nuts, low fat cheese and apple, mixed with a delicious homemade dressing. This snack lasts for two to three days in the fridge and could be nibbled on in place of the previous sugary snacks.

We talked about taking a little bit of time at weekends to plan meals for the week, and buying only the ingredients for those meals, so that there was no excuses such as not having what she needed to make the meal. I helped Tania to choose healthy meals that were simple to make, such as salmon with a zesty bean salad (tastes lovely and can be made in minutes), slow-cooked chicken in tarragon, a spicy fish dish and vegetable lasagne using aubergines instead of pasta, which could be used for two days' dinner. I could see the enthusiasm building up fast as Tania could see that she would be able to eat healthily but without spending too much time preparing the food. Her husband was easy to please, so she wouldn't be getting any argument from him!

The next thing we discussed was the need for Tania to be aware of what she was eating, rather than just mindlessly eating just to avoid hunger. I asked Tania to make sure that she ate her evening meal as early as possible, even if it occasionally meant eating before her husband, so that she had time to digest the food and relax before going to bed. I had taken a photo of Tania at her first visit (with her permission), and had sent that photo to her phone. I asked her to keep that photo in front of her while she was eating, to remind her of what she was moving away from. This helped Tania to keep her goal of being slimmer with more energy firmly in her mind while she was eating. The photo was there for her to look at any time she was tempted by sweet, sugary nutrition-empty food.

During the 'Weight off Your Plate' in-house programme that Tania was on with me, her husband had agreed that at weekends he would take the children out to give Tania some time to herself. I gave Tania a self-hypnosis script for her to learn and use as often as she could, as long as it was at least once a day. The self-hypnosis only took about ten minutes to do, but made the world of difference to Tania's previous lack of time out for herself, and to her focus on her goal.

By the end of the six-week programme, Tania had made all of the changes necessary to successfully take back control of her hectic lifestyle, and to lose weight in an enjoyable way. Her husband had kept to his word, and at weekends Tania would take the time to plan the following week's meals, together with her lunchtime snacks. The shopping was now being done online, with a definitive list written out beforehand, so there was no temptation of walking into the cake or sweet aisle at the supermarket. Tania was getting at least two nights' full sleep at weekends as her husband was seeing to the children, and she was pleased to report she had lost 11lbs in weight. A great start to a permanent lifestyle change which would ensure Tania continued to lose weight safely until she reached her target, and then to maintain the weight loss easily and effortlessly.

I hope you have enjoyed reading these ladies' success stories. You may have identified yourself somewhere along the line, but whatever your personal motivation for change is, you CAN do it!

You'll find some healthy and enjoyable food suggestions in chapter 9!

Here's to being Slim and Sassy!

Chapter Seven

TIPS AND TECHNIQUES FOR YOUR SUCCESS!

1. Find your personal motivation to lose weight!

There's little point in saying "I want to lose weight" without motivation, because you will find an excuse not to do it or you will start with good intentions, and then slip back into your old ways.

- What really drives you to want to change?
- Why now?
- Why haven't you done it before now?
- When was that moment that you decided enough was enough?
- What were you doing right at that moment?

Write your motivation down. How does it feel to you? Can you feel it physically in your body? Ask yourself, if you made the necessary changes, and you could never go back to your old ways, would you still do it? Be really honest with yourself, and unless the answer is a very firm YES, think again about your reasons for wanting successful weight loss now and focus on them.

You need to be absolutely 100 percent certain that you want to lose weight and keep the weight off above anything else right now. You need to have absolute determination without any traces of doubt that you WILL make lifestyle changes and keep with them, celebrating your success every step of the way. Every step you take away from your old ways which led you to being fat and unhappy is a step towards success.

So give yourself praise! You deserve it!

2. Identify those personal triggers and work to eliminate them!

We looked at personal triggers in Chapter Two. Look for them, identify them, and write them down. If you find yourself being triggered, say to yourself in a very loud and commanding voice (out loud or in your mind) STOP! FAT OFF TO THE OLD WAYS! I AM NOT GOING TO BE FAT ANY MORE!

If unresolved emotions are among your triggers, deal with them. Talk to someone, preferably someone who is not involved in your life, such as a professional therapist. If you're using food to push down those emotions no amount of dieting will help you lose weight successfully in the long term. If you keep doing the same as you've always done, you will always get what you've always got!

If your environment contains your triggers, change it! Remove temptation from your shopping list, and from your kitchen or wherever else you may have food (yes, even the place you may be hiding that bar of chocolate!). If you eat in your car or office, clear it all away and notice how clean everything looks now.

Change the place(s) where you eat. If you're habit is to eat from a tray in front of the TV- MOVE! Do you have a table and chair(s)? Try eating there instead. Changing just one thing like this gives your mind the powerful message that the old, outdated habits are changing!

If you enjoy wine, have a treat a couple of times a week by pouring yourself a small (125ml) glass to have with your evening meal. If you find yourself eyeing up the bottle for more, say to the wine "YOU'RE JUST ADDING TO MY WEIGHT, SO FAT OFF TO ANY MORE TODAY!"

Eat in front of a mirror – that can be a real wakeup call if you suddenly see yourself from the outside eating more than you need!

Keep that 'fat photo' of you on your phone in front of you when you eat. Better still, make a collage that shows the fat you, and also photos of when you were slimmer. If you have never been slim, cut out a realistic picture from a magazine (not a stick insect airbrushed model photo!), and put a head photo of you on top of it.

Add in pictures of perhaps a holiday destination you'd love to go to, or a bikini you know you will be wearing on the next beach you visit in the sun. Add pictures of your favourite perfume, make up, hairstyles – all of things that give you a lift and make you the sassy woman you are! Put copies of the collage everywhere, especially on the mirror! This is your goal and will become your reality, because you can make it happen!

Buy an item of clothing that you really like but in a size smaller than you are now. Hang it up on your wardrobe and look at it every day.

Tell yourself that you WILL be wearing that very soon, and have a goal date/event in the near future. This is a step towards wearing that item that you've already bought to wear when you're at your goal weight!

If someone cooks some yummy cakes or other treats, you don't have to eat them you know! You can politely say how wonderful they look, but you're not hungry right now. If they keep insisting, ask them to wrap one for you to take home. When you get home, enjoy half if it (only one treat here!) and share the rest with your partner (or the dog!). You're not offending anyone, because they won't know. If your trigger is the smell of the baker's shop, or the takeaway as you walk past, go a different way!

If you eat out at a restaurant, make a point of choosing something that you really enjoy, and leave one quarter of it on your plate.

If you have a dessert at a restaurant, eat it slowly and really appreciate the sweetness, then either leave a third of it, or share it with your partner!

When eating at home, have a special dinner plate that is smaller than your other dinner plates.

If you shop online, make a list before you start and stick to it. Congratulate yourself on shopping for healthy food. Plan your meals and snacks for the following week before you plan your list.

If you shop in a supermarket, go straight to the fruit and veg aisle first, and ignore the sweets, snacks and cakes aisles. Also ignore aisles that have frozen desserts. Imagine the signs above the aisles have big bold neon letters saying 'THIS WAY IF YOU WANT TO STAY FAT'.

If being too busy is your trigger for reaching for those unhealthy snacks and microwaved ready meals, planning your meals and snacks as above and buying only what you need for the week will take away that temptation.

You weren't too busy to be fat, so there's no excuse of being too busy to be slim!

If you feel hungry when you go to bed, pour yourself a glass of iced water with a slice of lemon. Keep it next to your bed and sip it slowly. Concentrate on the refreshing feel of the water in your mouth as opposed to something stodgy that sticks to the roof of your mouth!

Drink at least 6-8 glasses of water every day, and always when you start to feel hungry. You might be in need of hydration rather than food, so make it a habit to reach for that glass before you reach for the food!

If your workplace is cake time when it's someone birthday, offer to make some healthy treats as a contribution, then enjoy them with your colleagues.

If someone buys you a gift of chocolates or sweets, say a huge thank you and make a note to gift recycle them later!

Write down all of your excuses about being fat. Say them out loud as if you are justifying them to someone else. Imagine you are the other person – what would you say in response to your excuses?

Once you've gone through all of your excuses as above, tear up the paper or put it in the shredder. Excuses aren't worth the paper they're written on, because they'll only keep you fat!

3. RAISE THAT SELF-ESTEEM!

If you're feeling anxious and find yourself tempted to reach for comfort food, make a point of walking into another room and doing something different that's enjoyable, such as a spray of your favourite perfume, or putting on some lippy (yes, even if you're at home on your own!). Remember that new outfit you've bought that's hanging on the outside of your wardrobe? Pick it up and put it up against you. Look in the mirror and SMILE! Congratulate yourself on the fact that you've just taken steps towards a slimmer you in that gorgeous outfit!

Act as if! Walk with a positive posture, as if you are already that slimmer, confident, gorgeous woman you know you are inside. Think like a healthy eating slim person who wouldn't dream of eating sugary, fatty foods which will wreck her beautiful figure!

Make a point of doing something nice for yourself regularly.

You might choose a massage, beauty treatment, haircut/ new hair colour, new make-up, having your nails done, buying some pretty underwear, new shoes, new bag – or anything else you can think of. If the cost is an issue, get together with your daughter/sister/mum/best friend/neighbour and organise a pamper party once a month where you all give each other home treatments. You might even find you have a talent for making pamper treats such as face masks and lip balm out of your kitchen cupboard contents!

Have a favourite song that's really upbeat and strong, and dance and sing along to it! Tell yourself that the song is helping to melt away the fat as it gives you energy and motivates you to move that gorgeous body!

Make a point of looking in the mirror each morning when you get up and telling yourself you are gorgeous! SMILE at your reflection, and feel your self-esteem rising up!

Give compliments to others – you soon find you get some back!

Every day write down three things that you really like and appreciate about yourself and your life. Everyone has something, so I don't want to hear 'I can't think of anything'!!

Keep a journal of success. At the end of every day, write down what you've done that day towards being slim, healthy and gorgeous! It doesn't matter how small it is, every little thing you do towards shedding that fat and revealing the beautiful, sassy woman underneath is more precious than diamonds.

Share your successes with others. Talk about your journey of weight loss, share your experiences and give tips and suggestions to others if they're not sure which way to go.

Celebrate who you are! You are a wonderful, beautiful, energetic and clever woman – go out and share that with the world!

4. You can still have little treats while losing weight

If you eat healthily for 80% of the time, you can enjoy a little treat during the other 20 percent of the time. I learned this principle from weight loss expert Steve Miller, and it works brilliantly. Remember, you are the only one who is responsible for your choices, no one else! Losing weight permanently by way of lifestyle changes doesn't have the restrictions and dictations of a diet, so it's good to know that you can have that small piece of cake or small portion of takeaway at the weekend isn't it? Something to look forward to, and no-one is going to leap up and tell you it's wrong! It's about portion control, and the old saying 'a little of what you fancy does you good' is so true. The rest of the time you're eating healthily so reward yourself if you want to. Whatever your chosen treat, get into the habit of enjoying a small amount and really savouring the flavour and texture. Think about what you're eating!

5. Divide your plate into quarters and leave one quarter on your plate.

This is an easy habit to get into. You can still enjoy the food, but by leaving just 25% of what's on your plate, you are really making a difference to the calorific impact of the food. Congratulate yourself every time you do this and tell yourself you will not be fat anymore because you're in control!

When you're eating at home, you can buy a special plate that's smaller than your other dinner plates for your main meal of the day. Buy a plate you really like and see it as a valuable and effective weight loss tool. If your special plate is in the dishwasher, use the 25 percent off method. Don't forget, by using a smaller plate you are also reducing the calorific intake, so either way will work for you.

Of course, eating outside of your own home means using the 25 percent method, or people might start to think you are a bit odd if you carry your own plate around with you! When putting food on your smaller plate at home, arrange the food in the same way you would on a larger plate – no sneakily piling the food upwards!

6. Know your fats

For a long time, diets have urged people to cut right down on fats, but it hasn't always been made clear which fats are actually good for you to eat for successful weight loss and good health.

You shouldn't avoid fat, as it's needed for healthy growth and development, energy, organ protection and nutrient absorption. Good fat also helps the body to burn fat!

To lose weight and stay healthy, aim to include the good fats in your daily intake of food. Oily fish, nuts and seeds, green leafy vegetables, olive oil, olives and super foods like avocados. These fats provide an excellent source of nutrients to give you energy, plus they add taste to your food! Have you ever munched on a fat free 'nutrition' bar, only to find it tastes like the box it came in?

A balanced, healthy diet will contain carbohydrates (complex), protein and good fat (unsaturated). If you have a diet with no fat at all, the fat burning processes in the liver won't be triggered, and existing fat in your body will be stored around your waist, hips and thighs. A moderate amount of good fats in food will keep you full for longer, aiding successful weight loss without the need to follow a restrictive diet.

Food is a source of pleasure, so make sure you eat what you enjoy, as it will also raise your serotonin levels to make you feel good.

Good fats also give you energy, so that exercise is a real pleasure, giving you a rush of feel good hormones as it helps to melt away the fat.

One final word about the good guys of the fat world. Fat

soluble vitamins, A,D,E, and K need fat to be absorbed by the body. In deficiency in these vitamins can not only lead to low energy, but also dry skin and hair, brittle nails and muscle stiffness. Gorgeous women like you don't want that!

7. Smile as you say 'No thank you'

We've talked about saying no to temptation that other people put in front of you. If you're someone who has been brought up to 'eat it all up', or 'there are people starving in the world so you must eat it', you may have found it hard to say no when someone has prepared some food that you've been offered, perhaps at a social gathering. It can be quite easy at a barbeque or buffet to pick out the healthy options, but if someone points out the wonderful cake they've made, or brings you a bowl of trifle, you don't want to hurt their feelings by just refusing do you?

The trick is to either a) just eat a small amount, or b) give the person your best smile and say 'no thank you, I'm really quite full with all the other lovely food I've tried'. There's a double edged compliment there to your host, and both of you can move on without feeling guilty or rejected!

A smile can go a thousand miles to making someone's day, and it tells your own brain that all is well, and you are happy. This releases the feel good hormones, raising your self-esteem even further, which will keep you away from craving that sugary, fatty food!

8. As you move from fatty to sassy, create a style that tells the world that you're here

Have you ever noticed that slim, confident women have a certain style? It could be casual, dressy, smart or even sporty, but there's always a style that says 'CONFIDENT'. Just as you've now learned to discover your own triggers for the old unhealthy ways, now's the time to find your inner style that really tells the world who you truly are. Maybe when you were fat you wore baggy clothes to cover up the bulges? Maybe you let your hair just hang in a less than flattering way, or pulled it back in a ponytail? Were those roots showing through because you couldn't be bothered to do anything about it during the fat times? Did you wear flat shoes because being sexy just wasn't you?

Hopefully by now you've got to know yourself a lot more than you did. Got to know that you have a brilliant mind full of your own personal resources to get your slimmer, healthier and gorgeous you revealed!

Whatever your current weight loss is, you can be really proud that the old ways were the result of old outdated habits and an unhealthy relationship with food and emotions, and you have now walked away from those old ways for good. FAT OFF TO THE OLD WAYS!

Think of yourself as an emerging beautiful butterfly. What are your colours? What style feels really good to you, true to who you really are? If you're a jeans and t-shirt kind of woman, you can treat yourself to some really sexy jeans and tops (maybe with some super sexy shoes too!), you will look and feel like a millions dollars, while still being comfortable with what you're wearing. Again, if money is an issue, why not search the Charity shops for some designer clothes? You might be surprised about what some people throw out!

The same goes for whatever your style. You may even find that what you thought was your style for years is not you at all. Perhaps the super sassy woman that's emerging has always been there but you hadn't met her before now!

Wearing what you feel really good in will give your confidence an extra boost, along with your slim and shapely body. If you've never worn make-up or perfume, try it and see!

If the spark had gone out of your relationship (or you're single and looking for love), the new you might just need that extra burst of energy that comes with being slim and healthy now you're looking and feeling so gorgeous!

One of my very successful weight loss ladies has taken to carrying around a simple lip gloss, and while she has that in her bag and on her lips she feels like the gorgeous woman she is. It doesn't have to be anything extravagant (unless you want it to be!), but whatever makes you feel good, and reflects the new slimmer, confident you will work wonders!

In the next chapter I'm going to give you some simple self-hypnosis techniques that you can use every day to maintain your successful lifestyle changes.

Here's to being Slim and Sassy!

Chapter Eight

SELF HYPNOSIS TECHNIQUES

Self-hypnosis is a brilliant way of reprogramming your mind away from outdated habits that made you fat into healthy eating, enjoyable exercise and successful weight loss. It's a motivational tool that you alone have direct access to and full use of!

In addition to some techniques for your successful weight loss, I am going to include a technique to help you to take time out and relax as you let your inner mind do the work. The weight loss self-hypnosis should be used at least once a day until you have reached your goal weight, and the relaxation technique can be used whenever you're feeling the need to give your mind a break from everyday 'busyness'.

You may like one more than the others at different times, so go with what feels good to you.

The motivational sessions for successful weight loss are quite short, and should take no more than 10-15 minutes to complete. They are easy to remember, and the more you practice the easier it becomes to simply slip into trance. The relaxation technique is longer, and you might like to read it through a few times, and then write down key words to remind you of the content. Another way of using this technique is to record the content and play it back to yourself.

IMPORTANT: Whenever you choose to use these self-hypnosis techniques please make sure it is safe to do so. Do not use when driving or operating machinery, or in any other situation where your full alertness is needed for the safety of you and others.

Successful weightloss techniques

First technique

Make sure your phone is switched off and you won't have any distractions for at least 15 minutes. Sit in a comfortable chair, feet on the floor, and hands in your lap.

Fix your eyes on a spot in front of you just above your eye level. As you keep your eyes focused on that spot, tell yourself that as your outer focus on that spot becomes hazy around the edges, your inner focus is becoming clearer. Keeping your eyes on that spot, tell yourself that you are going to count backwards from 10 to 1, and each number you count will be on your outbreath. Each number will take you deeper as it connects you to that inner focus.

Begin to count backwards from 10 to 1 on each outbreath, and notice how your eyes are becoming heavier as your mind becomes sharper. When you get to 1 allow your eyes to close if you want to.

In your own mind, in a strong voice, say these words:

- THE FAT IN MY BODY IS MELTING AWAY AS I CHOOSE TO EAT HEALTHY NUTRITIOUS FOOD
- THE SLIM, GORGEOUS WOMAN INSIDE IS EMERGING AS I TAKE BACK CONTROL OF FOOD
- I LOVE EXERCISE, AND I CAN FEEL IT BURNING OFF THE FAT WITH EVERY MOVEMENT
- AS I SAY THESE WORDS MY MOTIVATION TO BE SLIM IS ROCKETING !

Repeat the words over and over until it's time to return to the room. (Your mind will let you know when it's time to end the session, because you will have told yourself at the beginning that you will be coming back to the room in 10 or 15 minutes.) Count up from 1 to 10, and as you open your eyes at 10, get up and walk to the nearest mirror, smile at your reflection and say 'well done, you gorgeous woman'. Go and enjoy your day!

Second technique

Make sure your phone is switched off and you won't have any distractions for at least 15 minutes. Sit in a comfortable chair, feet on the floor and hands in your lap.

Focus your attention on your right wrist and imagine there is a helium balloon tied to it. As you focus on your wrist and hand, feel and see the balloon lifting your wrist up. At the same time raise your left arm to shoulder level, and imagine there is a bucket hanging on that arm, which is gradually being filled with sand. As the bucket is filled with sand your arm gets heavier and heavier, as your right arm gets lighter and lighter. When both arms are have a good distance between them count to 5 and as you do so, let both hands fall into your lap and say SLEEP as your eyes close.

Feel your focus rushing from the outside to the inside, as you see in your mind a very clear picture of the future you, slim, healthy and radiating a big smile. Notice what the future you is wearing, and how amazing you look. Listen as the future you tells you tells you how fantastic she feels, how she has so much energy and respect for herself. Listen as she tells you that she got to be slim and gorgeous by eating healthy, smaller portions and loving daily exercise.

As you feel a surge of motivation repeat these words using a very strong, determined inner voice:

- I AM IN CONTROL OF MY CHOICES
- I EAT ONLY WHEN I'M STOMACH HUNGRY
- I CHOOSE TO BE SLIM AND HEALTHY
- I AM NOT A MEMBER OF THE FAT CLUB ANY MORE

Repeat the words until your mind tells you it is time to come back to the room. Take a deep breath, feel the strong motivational surge in your mind as you open your eyes and return to the room. Stand up, walk to the nearest mirror and smile at your reflection. Tell your reflection "you are one amazing woman".

Third technique

Make sure your 'phone is switched off and you won't have any distractions for at least 15 minutes. Sit in a comfortable chair, feet on the floor and hands in your lap.

Focus your eyes on a spot in front of you, just above eye level. Keeping your eyes focused, notice 3 things in your peripheral vision, without taking your eyes off the spot in front of you. Using your inner voice, tell yourself what you see, for instance "I can see the window, the light and the table".
Go on to tell yourself 3 sounds you can hear.

Then 3 sensations you can feel. It might be your feet on the floor, your hands in your lap, or the warmth of the air in the room, for instance.

Repeat this with 2 things you can see, hear and feel and finally 1 thing.

When you've completed this, allow your eyes to close as you focus your attention on the following words as you say them to yourself in a strong, determined inner voice:

- I REJECT ALL FOODS THAT WOULD KEEP ME FAT
- I CAN SAY NO TO TEMPTATION AND FEEL GOOD ABOUT IT
- I EMBRACE MY BODY SHAPE AS IT CHANGES FROM FAT TO SLIM
- I AM TOO BEAUTIFUL TO BE FAT

Repeat the words until your mind tells you it is time to come back to the room. Take a deep breath, feel the strong motivational surge in your mind as you open your eyes and return to the room. Stand up, walk to the nearest mirror and smile at your reflection. Tell your reflection: "you are one gorgeous woman".

Fourth technique

Make sure your 'phone is switched off and you won't have any distractions for at least 15 minutes. Sit in a comfortable chair, feet on the floor and hands in your lap.

See the words 'CALM AND FOCUSED' in front of you, notice the size and shape of the letters and feel the meaning of the words washing over you as you feel your mind becoming calm and focused on your inner motivation to ditch the fat and get gorgeous!

Allow any other sounds in your environment to merge into this experience, as you choose to focus your attention completely on the image of the fat in your body melting away to reveal the beautiful slim woman underneath the layers. (It is good to have your eyes closed at this point so that your inner focus is total). See a very clear image of yourself becoming slimmer and slimmer as your confidence soars higher and higher. Feel that surge of confidence wrapping itself around you as you say these words to yourself in a very determined and strong inner voice:

- I WILL NEVER BE FAT AGAIN
- I CAN FEEL THE FAT DISSOLVING AS I SEE MYSELF AS SLIM AND GORGEOUS
- I AM IN FULL CONTROL OF FOOD
- I AM THE ONLY PERSON RESPONSIBLE FOR LETTING MYSELF GET FAT IN THE PAST
- I AM MOTIVATED AND STRONG AND I WILL NOT BE HELD TO RANSOM BY FOOD

Repeat the words until your mind tells you it is time to come back to the room. Take a deep breath, feel the strong motivational surge in your mind as you open your eyes and return to the room. Stand up, walk to the nearest mirror and smile at your reflection. Tell your reflection “you are stunning and I love this reflection”.

Self hypnosis for deep relaxation

For this type of self-hypnosis, it is OK to lie down if you prefer that to sitting, so that your body can relax physically while your subconscious mind can travel to a calm place. Remember to switch off your phone and make sure you will not be disturbed, and to make sure it is safe for you to do this.

This should take about 20-25 minutes or so and the more you practice the easier it will be to remember. It is personal to you, so once you've done it a couple of times you will be able to slip straight into a relaxed frame of mind whenever you feel the need for time out. As suggested earlier, you can choose to record the words, or simply get a feel for the overall experience with key words to remind you when you first start.

As you lie/sit there in this safe and comfortable place, you can be sure your physical body will respond to these words and images by becoming deeply relaxed, while you can travel to a different place in your mind where you can discover your own inner resources.

Take a moment to be aware of your breathing. Just breathe at a comfortable pace that feels natural and right for you, and as you do so you might notice that there is a moment when you feel any tension or tightness dissolving away from your muscles and joints.

I don't know whether this moment will be right now, in the next couple of minutes or whether you will become aware of it at a later point, but you'll feel it. When you feel your body relax like that as tension is released, you will notice that your inner focus has become very clear. It's as if you have flicked two switches in the control centre of your mind – one to switch off tension and anxiety and the other to switch on clarity and openness in your subconscious mind. See those switches now.

Some people feel as if their body has become so relaxed it feels heavy, while others feel as if they're floating on air. I wonder which one you will feel as these changes occur now?

As your inner focus is now so clear, I want you to count backwards in your mind from 10 to 1, saying each number in your mind on your outbreaths.

With each number you count, feel yourself travelling deeper and deeper into your innermost mind, that part of you that knows exactly how to be calm and focused, as you let go of everyday thoughts and cares.

When you reach the number 1, take a deep breath, and as you exhale see a large bright number 0 in your mind as you feel yourself going deeper into calm. Notice how the colour of the zero draws you into it.

Step through that zero to the other side. You're now in a place that feels very, very relaxing and calm to you. It might be a place that is familiar to you, or it might be a place that your powerful imagination is showing you. In this place, you feel safe and secure, calm and relaxed. This is your place that you can come to whenever you want to take time out from a busy day.

It is also a place where positive change can take place, because you can see everything so clearly here. Take a moment to do whatever you need to do to make this place even more comfortable for you before finding a place to sit and feel the calm clarity washing over you.

In this place is everything you need to let go of anxiety and stress and to use your own inner resources to successfully lose weight and raise your self-esteem.

Take a few moments to notice resources that perhaps you were previously unaware of, or had forgotten about.

These resources can be objects, thoughts or memories, or it could be a person who will support you on your journey, but whatever your own resources are, see them clearly now.

While your mind is so clear, you can find a new understanding of yourself. Things that previously used to bother you will from now on just wash over you as you move forward towards your goal of successful weight loss and confidence.

Take as long as you need now to use your own inner resources to your best advantage. In this place, you will find your inner voice is strong and determined, as you listen carefully to what your mind is telling you.

Each time you visit this place, you will find your inner strength and determination grow stronger, because your mind will let you know what is needed for you to successfully lose the unwanted fat and become the confident, slim woman you are inside.

When you are sure you have completed what you need to do today in this place, count yourself up and back to the room, using 1-10. Do this faster than when you counted yourself down into hypnosis.

As you reach number 10, open your eyes, have a stretch and wiggle your fingers and toes. Get up, walk to the nearest mirror and give your reflection the widest smile you have! Enjoy the rest of your day.

I hope you enjoy using these self-hypnosis techniques.

Here's to being Slim and Sassy!

Chapter Nine

SOME SUGGESTIONS FOR MEALS AND SNACKS

As mentioned earlier in this book, eating healthily for 80 percent of the time and enjoying a little of what you fancy 20 percent of the time enables successful weight loss without restrictions. There's nothing worse than feeling you can't enjoy the taste of something you like because it's on a 'banned' list somewhere!

As humans, we use food as a source of pleasure as well as for nourishment, which is one reason diets don't work long term. Nobody likes to be told they can't have something they really like, do they?

You don't need me to tell you that it's important to have a balance in your diet of slow-release carbohydrates, good fats, lean protein and low-fat dairy products. Cutting out carbs completely is a mistake that a lot of people have made in the past with some crazy diets, but if you don't have carbs you will be lacking in energy, which can lead to a 'can't be bothered' approach to exercise, craving for comfort food and weight gain! So let's look at the good guys when it comes to carbohydrates:

Anything that has a slow release of glucose into the bloodstream will stop you feeling hungry. So long as you are mindful of your portion sizes (no massive bowls of pasta please!), you can enjoy filling food without the guilt. Before I give you the list, please ditch any white bread or white rice, pastries and pasta as these will raise your sugar levels quickly, and the inevitable crash in energy will follow.

Good carbs and fibre sources that will give you energy and a healthy digestive tract:

- Quinoa
- Whole wheat pasta
- Brown rice
- Beans and lentils
- Oats
- Vegetables
- Wholemeal bread, preferably with wholegrains (check labels for sugar!)
- Barley
- Squash
- Dates
- Low fat cheese (also on protein list)
- Low fat greek yoghurt (check sugar levels)
- Peanuts (not salted)
- Raisins
- Sweet potatoes
- Potatoes in their skins
- Fruit (some fruits are higher in natural sugar than others, but they won't cause a spike in your blood sugar levels)

Good proteins:

- Low fat cheese
- Eggs
- Semi skimmed milk (remember milk contains lactose, so not too much!)
- Soya products
- Lean meat
- Fish
- Nuts and seeds
- Humus (small amount)
- Peanut butter (watch out for the sugar!)
- Tofu

Good fats:

- Olive oil (good source of Omega 9)
- Sunflower oil
- Sesame oil
- Rapeseed oil
- Evening primrose oil
- Soya oil
- Vegetable oil
- Omega 3 (as well as oils, this can be found in flaxseed, chia seeds, oily fish, hemp, walnuts, pistachios, brazil nuts, sesame seeds, pumpkin seeds, avocados, dark green leafy vegetables)

I'm sure you'll come up with your own mixes for snacks and meals, but here's a few that I've tried and really enjoyed, without putting on an ounce!

Breakfast:

Warm fruit salad:
Take a mixture of your favourite dried fruits, such as apricots, prunes, dates and figs, and mix with a small amount of apple juice. Warm through in a saucepan, put in a small bowl and drizzle over some low fat natural yoghurt and runny honey. Sprinkle a few chia, pumpkin or sunflower seeds on top and enjoy. Remember there is sugar in dried fruit, and also in honey, so a small bowl is enough to give you that happily full feeling!

Homemade Granola:
100 ml sunflower oil
20 ml malt extract
50 ml runny honey
320g rolled oats
250g large flakes oat flakes
40g hazelnuts and almonds
25g desiccated coconut
75g seed mix (sunflower, pumpkin and sesame seeds)

This does have a fair amount of natural sugar (not refined), but will give you a real energy boost for the whole morning! A small bowl is all you need to give you a real energy boost for the morning.

In a saucepan, mix together 100ml sunflower oil, 50 ml of runny honey and 20 ml of malt extract. Heat gently, stirring constantly until nice and runny. Mix in all the remaining ingredients and pour into a small roasting dish. Cook for about 20 minutes at 190c/375f, then remove from the oven and allow to cool. When it's cool, you can break it apart with a fork, and add in some fruit such as blueberries. Store in an airtight container, and serve with a splash of natural yoghurt.

Homemade Apple Muesli:
4oz rolled oats
2oz sunflower or pumpkin seeds
1 tablespoon runny honey
½ pint water
Handful of red grapes
Handful of toasted flaked almonds
Handful of hazelnuts
2 medium sized apples, thinly sliced
Teaspoon of cinnamon
Grated rind of an orange

Soak the oats and seeds overnight in the water, then mix in the remaining ingredients. You could try different fruits, such as banana, plums or apricots. Enjoy a small bowl with a spoonful of natural low fat yoghurt.

Cheesy eggs:
In a non-stick saucepan, add a dash of olive oil and a very small piece of butter. Scramble 3 eggs, and add a pinch of hot paprika, salt and black pepper. Scramble the eggs in the pan, and just before they're done, add in a small handful of low fat grated cheese. If you're really hungry, top the mixture on a slice of wholemeal toast.

A variation on cheesy eggs is spinach eggs, where you replace the cheese with some dry fried spinach.

Lunch:

Butternut squash and carrot soup with chilli:
In a large pan, add 1 tbsp. of olive oil and heat gently. Add in a butternut squash, cut into chunks. (Waitrose sell this already done for you!). Grate in 3 carrots, and 1 medium sized potato. Add a squirt of runny honey, and a handful of raisins,

then a pinch of dried chilli flakes, salt and black pepper to taste. Add a generous sprinkle of Boullion low salt stock powder, and top up with water to desired level. Remember, the less water you add in, the thicker the soup will be.

Simmer until the vegetables are soft (the potatoes and carrots take the longest time), then blitz. Serve with a swirl of natural low fat yoghurt and a sprig of coriander – enjoy!

If you're very peckish (although this is very filling), add in a couple of wholemeal crispbreads.

Quick salad bowl:

Cut up one stick of celery, two cherry tomatoes, 2 dried apricots and an apple (Braeburn are good for this). Add in a small handful of sultanas, and some low fat grated cheese or light salad cheese. In a separate bowl, mix together a generous helping of low fat mayonnaise with some lemon juice and about 2-3 teaspoons of dried tarragon. Add salt and black pepper to taste. Pour over the dry ingredients and mix thoroughly. This mix will last for two to three days in an airtight container in the fridge. Delicious and filling!

Rustic Bean Salad:

I packet rocket, ready washed
4 tomatoes, skinned and chopped.
Can of mixed salad beans, drained and washed.
I chopped red onion
I celery stick, chopped
Handful of your favourite olives (pitted)
3 tablespoons of lemon juice
Pinch of dried chilli flakes
Salt and black pepper to taste
I tablespoon of red wine vinegar
Can tuna in spring water
1 tablespoon olive oil

Mix all ingredients together, adjust seasoning to taste and serve with a sprig of coriander and small wholemeal pitta bread

Snacks:

Chilli Pitta crisps:
Take two or three wholemeal pitta breads and tear them roughly into chunks. Lightly oil a baking tray, and scatter the pitta pieces over.

Lightly spray with olive oil, and sprinkle with dried chilli flakes, paprika and a little salt to taste. Bake at 190c for about ten minutes. Allow to cool and enjoy with the next recipe for red pepper salsa!

Red Pepper Salsa:
1 large red pepper, halved, oiled and grilled for 10 minutes until charred. ½ tablespoon of balsamic vinegar. Small pinch of sugar and 1 tablespoon of olive oil.

De-seed and chop the cooked pepper and blend in a processor with the vinegar and sugar. Transfer to a fresh bowl and stir in the oil, and salt and black pepper to taste.

Spicy Sweet Potato wedges with homemade humus:
Cut one or two large sweet potatoes into wedges, keeping the skin on (the skin adds nutrients such as potassium and fibre). Lightly oil a baking tray, and arrange the wedges on it. Spray the wedges with olive oil, and sprinkle with hot paprika and a little sea salt. Bake in oven at 200c for about 35 minutes until soft.

Meanwhile blend together one 400g tin of chick peas, drained and washed, the juice of a lemon, 4 tablespoons of extra virgin olive oil, 1 large garlic clove, crushed, sea salt and ground black pepper to taste, and a bunch of fresh herbs to your taste (basil or coriander are both delicious).

You could mix and match the dips – salsa with this and humus with the pitta bread crisps.

Chicken and feta bites:

Grill 2 lean chicken breasts, skin removed. Remove when browned and place to one side.

Meanwhile, mix together in a bowl light (low fat) feta cheese, chopped olives (your favourite flavour), and a small amount of ricotta cheese. Season with salt and ground black pepper, and add in a handful of chopped basil. You could also add in some dry fried spinach to that extra zing!

Slice the chicken breast and arrange on a plate closely together, with the mixture spread along the top. A small side salad is lovely with this, or a tangy rocket and orange zest salad (literally just rocket and orange zest, with a small drizzle of balsamic).

Basil tomatoes on toast:

While toasting a slice of wholemeal bread, add a small amount of olive oil to a non-stick pan, and lightly fry halved cherry or plum tomatoes. Add salt and black pepper to taste, together with a handful of torn basil leaves. Enjoy!

Dinner:

Mediterranean Fish Stew:

2 tablespoons olive oil or sunflower oil.
2 red onions, chopped.
2 carrots, roughly sliced.
3 celery sticks, chopped
2 large garlic cloves, crushed
4 large chopped and skinned tomatoes
1 pint vegetable stock (Bouillon low salt)

2 teaspoons fish sauce
¾ pint dry white wine (no calories from this as the cooking process evaporates the alcohol)
8oz peeled king prawns
1lb cod fillets
½ lbs haddock fillets
Mussels (amount to your personal taste)
I bay leaf
2tbs tomato puree
Salt and ground black pepper to taste

Heat the oil in a large pan, and add the celery, onions, carrots, garlic, tomato puree and tomatoes. Cook until softened, and add the wine, stock and bay leaf. Simmer to let the flavours absorb.

Add the cod and haddock (cut into chunks), simmer for about 20 minutes on low heat, then add the prawns and mussels if including. Season to taste.

You could replace the fish with chicken if you prefer.

Serve in a bowl with a slice of wholemeal crusty bread and a small glass of white wine. Delicious!

Healthy chicken curry:
2 tablespoons olive oil
2 red onions, roughly chopped
5 garlic cloves, crushed
400g red lentils or pack of ready cooked puy lentils
600 ml vegetable stock (Bouillon low salt)
Bunch of fresh coriander
5 skinless cooked chicken breasts cut into chunks. (You can buy ready cooked and sliced chicken breast in supermarkets if you're pushed for time)
2-3 tablespoons of curry paste (you may prefer a madras or a milder korma heat level, so I'll leave this ingredient for you

to decide!)
Small handful of dried chopped apricots and sultanas for sweetness
Sea salt and black pepper to taste
Whole packet of baby spinach

Cook lentils according to instructions if using red lentils. Heat some of the oil in a large saucepan and fry off the onions and garlic.

Add cooked lentils and chicken, together with the curry paste and stir. Simmer, and add stock as you stir. Add the spinach at the end of cooking.

Adjust seasoning to taste.

Serve in a bowl with a swirl of low fat natural yoghurt and some fresh coriander.

Spicy Fish Dish:
1 tin chopped tomatoes
2 teaspoons of preserved lemon paste, or 8 preserved lemon slices
1.5 teaspoons of harissa paste
Salt and ground black pepper
3 cloves of garlic, crushed
1 tin anchovy fillets
Handful of olives (chili stuffed olives work really well with this)
2 Basa fillets (you can replace with lean chicken breasts if you prefer)
Mix together all the ingredients.
Place the fish (or chicken) in a roasting dish, and cover with the mixed ingredients.
Cover with tin foil and bake in a hot oven for about 35 minutes (if using chicken make sure the fillets are not too thick)
Serve with brown rice and quinoa.

Desserts:

Banana and Apricot Bowl:
2 bananas
4oz dried apricots
2oz raisins
2 teaspoons of lemon juice
150ml low fat natural yoghurt
Honey to taste
Crushed pine nuts
Ground cinnamon
Mix fruits together with lemon juice. Arrange in dishes and pour over honey then the natural yoghurt, nuts and ground cinnamon.

Passion fruit and fig yoghurt:
250ml low fat Greek yoghurt
3 passion fruits
1 tablespoon runny honey
4 fresh figs
Mint to decorate

Cut the passion fruit in half, and scoop out the seeds and mix with the honey and yoghurt. Cut each fig into four segments, and then cover with the yoghurt mixture. Decorate with a sprig of mint before serving.

Treats:

This chapter wouldn't be complete without some suggestions for treats. After all, you are eating healthy food for at least 80 percent of the time aren't you?!

Do bear in mind that these treats contain some fattening ingredients, so enjoy a small amount, eat it slowly, and really appreciate those flavours!

Orange Nut Flapjacks:
125g butter
30g demerara sugar
2 tablespoons runny honey
180g rolled oats
30g chopped nuts of your choice
Grated rind of 1 large orange
Handful of dried cranberries

Heat the butter, sugar and honey in a saucepan over a low heat until the ingredients are melted and blended. Remove from heat.
Stir in the oats, orange rind, cranberries and nuts. Mix well and spoon into a lightly oiled 7 inch tin, pressing down lightly. Bake in a pre-heated oven at 180c for 30 minutes. Loosen the sides while still warm. When cool, turn out and cut into squares. Enjoy a square as a treat. The remainder will keep in an airtight container for a few days.

Sultana and Orange Fruit Loaf:
50g butter
1 teaspoon bicarbonate of soda
200 ml skimmed milk
200g wholemeal flour
25g Allbran
Half teaspoon ground cinnamon
250g sultanas
100g soft brown sugar
Granted rind of one large orange
50g crushed walnuts

50g chopped dates
3 tablespoons orange juice

Blend the milk with the bicarbonate of soda in a mixing bowl. Add the remaining ingredients and mix well. Line a 1 lb loaf tin with greaseproof paper and spoon the mixture in. Bake at 160c for 2 hours. Remove from oven and allow to cool.
You can decorate the top with low fat cream cheese mixed with crushed nuts and orange peel, or brush with melted orange marmalade. Enjoy a slice as your treat.

I hope these suggestions will prove enjoyable for you, and it gives you an idea of how delicious healthy food can be – be adventurous, and make up your own scrap book of your favourite recipes for healthy weight loss!
Here's to being Slim and Sassy!

Chapter Ten

DAILY CHECKLIST FOR HEALTHY WEIGHT LOSS

I want to end the book with a few reminders for your daily journey to successful weight loss and higher confidence. Each one is important on its own, and collectively they will give you a daily checklist to motivate and inspire you towards your healthy goal. So here is my Top 40.

1.When you wake up, have a good stretch, and say to yourself: "Today is a Fat Off day and everything I do today will keep me on my road towards being Slim and Sassy". When you get up, go to the nearest mirror, smile your biggest smile at your reflection and tell yourself that you are one gorgeous woman!

2.It is always a great idea to exercise before breakfast if you can, because your body will burn off fat as you haven't eaten any carbs yet. Choose something that you really enjoy. Dig out those fitness DVDs, take the dog for a long walk, join a gym, go for a swim, or run up and down the stairs a few times until your heart responds to the cardio workout, and you are feeling comfortably warm and slightly out of breath.

3.When you've exercised, congratulate yourself that you've just melted away more of your unwanted onesie of fat.

4.Find ways each day to increase your exercise, and make sure you enjoy doing it! Whatever your daily environment is, you can find ways to include more movement into your day, no excuses! Every movement is melting that fat away!

5.Even if you're not going out, wear something that makes you feel good, put your lippy on, a spray of perfume and do your hair. I guarantee doing that will make you feel good about yourself. If you dress to slob about, that's exactly how you'll feel, and being a slob is not for you, is it?!

6.Avoid sugary breakfast cereals, and choose fruit and natural yoghurt, natural oats or a protein dish such as scrambled eggs and spinach. What you eat for breakfast will create your energy levels and mood stability throughout the day, so choose wisely! You know what sugar can do to you don't you! It may be sweet, but it's not your friend!

7.Have activities that you enjoy that don't involve food. Wherever you are, whether it's at home or work, create space for fun! It might just be 10 minutes playing with your dog, or time out of the office walking around the building, but it's YOU time – very important for your motivation!

8.If you're feeling anxious or stressed, use 'square breathing' to quickly feel calm again. You can do this anywhere that it's safe to do so, and it only takes a few minutes. Imagine a large square, and notice that the square is of a colour that means calm to you. Visualise moving up the left hand side of the square as you breathe in to the count of 4, then along the top of the square left to right as you hold the breath for the count of 4, down the right side of the square as you breathe out to the count of 4, and along the bottom line of the square right to left, as you pause to the count of 4. Repeat this a few times until you notice yourself feeling calmer and calmer. Smile your best smile, and enjoy the rest of your day.

9.Remember to eat only when you're stomach hungry. Drink a glass of water first, then if you're still hungry after 10 minutes chances are you need refuelling!

10.Choose a light lunch that's easy to make, filling and energy giving. Something like a bean salad with an avocado, chilli and lime dressing will be a real powerhouse of energy without adding to your waistline. If you're in a rush, chop up some fruit with some low fat crème fraiche and a sprinkling of chopped nuts – delicious and nutritious!

11.If you find yourself making excuses like "I haven't got time for breakfast/lunch/dinner" STOP!! No more excuses. You need to maintain your blood sugar levels throughout the day, or your energy will crash, and you will be guaranteed to start craving something fast, sugary and/or greasy.

12.Eat small healthy snacks in between meals to keep that blood sugar stable. Some suggestions are a handful of nuts, a chopped up apple, a few grapes, slices of melon or kiwi, pitta crisps (see recipe in Chapter 9) with perhaps a small piece of low fat hard cheese, a smoothie full of fruit and/or vegetables, made with half light almond or coconut milk and half water, or a healthy home-made dip with carrot or celery sticks. I'm sure you will be making up your own favourite snacks, but whatever you choose, think about not only your weight, but also your energy and mood.

13.Use a smaller than average plate for your main meal, or cover only 80% of a normal sized plate (no piling upwards!). Alternatively as suggested earlier in this book, you can choose to leave 25% on the plate – nothing is ever truly wasted, as everything eventually becomes recycled, so ditch the guilt if you choose this method.

14.Eat slowly and mindfully, and really appreciate the flavours, textures, colours and aromas of the food.

15.Put your knife and fork down while you're chewing each mouthful of food.

16.Have your 'fat photo' on your phone and look at it while you're eating. Make a collage of fat photos of you, and also photos of when you were slimmer, together with your favourite holiday destination (if you haven't yet been, just imagine), your favourite shoes, perfume, dress and anything else that motivates you and drives you forward. Keep a copy of the collage in the places where you prepare food and eat and keep a copy on your phone to remind you of how you were at the beginning of your journey, and what you're aiming for.

17.Buy clothes that are one or two sizes smaller than you wore at the start of your journey, and hang them up on the front of your wardrobe. Every day look at the clothes and smile, as you tell them "I'll be wearing you very soon".

18.Keep a daily journal. Divide it into sections (or buy more than one journal) for daily food and drink, how you feel each day, what exercise you've done, what you will be doing tomorrow towards your healthy weight loss goal, and a daily celebration of success. Every day will be a success for you because you're taking positive steps towards melting that fat off, so no excuses about what to write please!

19.Tell a good friend what you're doing and why. If you can, find a friend who will be alongside you on your journey so that you can motivate each other. Make a point of texting or talking to each other every day to give each other encouragement. You might even consider getting a group of friends together who want to lose weight successfully. Arrange weekly get togethers, where you can share your successes and recipes. You could each put in a contribution and buy a 'prize' for the first person to lose their first stone. You'll be surprised at how a little competition can really motivate you!

20.Every day, make a point of looking online for new healthy recipes, and build your own personal recipe book of things you really enjoy.

21.Drink 6-8 glass of water each day. If you find water boring, try adding in a slice of lemon and some ice.

22.Be aware of your ideal sleep time that ensures you wake up feeling refreshed and energised. Some people need a full 8-10 hours, while others are raring to go after 5 hours, so once you've worked out what your personal sleep needs are, make sure you aim for that every night.

23.Avoid TV, energising music, arguments, phone calls, caffeine, alcohol and eating before bedtime, as all of these things will disrupt your sleep.

24.Keep a glass of iced water with lemon next to your bed to keep you hydrated if you wake up feeling hungry during the night.

25.Avoid hidden saboteurs! The person at work who brings in cakes, the sweet trolley at work, the 'this way if you want to stay fat' aisles in the supermarket, the relative who brings you a box of chocolates, the buffet tables full of tempting food, the barbeque host who tells you they've spent ages preparing the food, the smell of the bakers as you walk past, the cupcakes on special offer – you can probably extend this list! The words 'NO! I WILL NOT BE FAT ANY MORE!' should be at the ready in your mind when faced with temptation.

26.Don't get hung up on weighing yourself. Once a week maximum is OK, but if you prefer to know you're melting the fat by the way your clothes are becoming looser, that's also OK.

27.Be aware of your posture. By standing tall and holding your head high, you're giving your brain and the world the message that you're feeling great – and you will!

28.When you're eating out, see it as a treat, so if you are ordering three courses, make two of them the healthier option. Stick to the plan of eating only 75% of what's on your plate, and enjoy the whole experience, not just the food and drink.

29.Be aware of the amount of sugar in alcoholic and soft drinks. That extra glass of wine might just tip your scales the wrong way. Tell yourself how many glasses of wine you're going to enjoy on a social occasion, and congratulate yourself for sticking to it.

30.Spend time each day really imagining that future, slimmer you. See that image, imagine stepping into it and feeling how good it feels to have said goodbye to all that fat. Imagine running your hands down your hips and getting a real rush of pride and enthusiasm as you feel slim and sexy in place of fat and frumpy!

31.Feed your style, not your stomach. If you used to dress in a frumpy, unflattering way when you were fat, walk past those clothes shops now and smile – they don't belong in your world!

32.Empty your wardrobe of all clothes that don't make you feel good when you wear them – ditch the dross!! You are way too gorgeous to wear dross clothes! Same goes for your shoes, bags and make up, even your hairstyle. Outdated you is out – new slim and gorgeous you is in!

33.Ditch the diet books! You don't need them because you know exactly how to be slim and gorgeous don't you? Who needs a diet book telling you you're not allowed to eat a little of what you fancy!

34.Get creative with your cooking. Make it your mission to be inspirational to your family and friends as you cook healthy, nutritious foods. Tell the world what you've discovered!

35.Start a Facebook page if you're into social media, telling people about your journey from fatty to slim and gorgeous. Tweet about your daily successes – your success can inspire others to get up off their lazy backsides and do something about their weight right now! You are doing it, and there's nothing like someone else's success story or daily posts and blogs to give others motivation.

36.Enjoy experimenting with what feels good in your life, from eating healthy food to wearing clothes that feel great, and maybe even spicing up your relationship. If you're not in a relationship at the moment, enjoy the 'you' time, and when you're ready, go out and wow the world! You won't be on your own for long with your new confidence and gorgeous look!

37.Smile, laugh with people who matter to you, enjoy your life and the fact that you are who you are!

38.Longer term: plan realistic weightloss interim targets. For instance, if your overall goal is to be 4st lighter, have 1st goals, together with a realistic time frame in which you're going to reach that goal.

39.Longer term: When you reach each of your interim goals, celebrate! Treat yourself to something affordable that you really want, and send yourself a congratulations card! I encourage clients to send themselves flowers (of course with an explanation to their husbands as to where they came from!!).

40.Longer term: When you reach your ultimate goal, do something that you've always wanted to do, and sing from the rooftops that you've done it!

I hope you've enjoyed reading this little book, and found some inspiration in here to get you started towards letting go of old emotions, melting away the fat and finding the slim, gorgeous and unique woman you are!

To your great success,

Lynda x

Want to know more?

I hope you've found this little book helpful, and I would love to hear from you with your stories at www.hypnotherapysoutheast.co.uk. You are also very welcome to post your questions on my Facebook page at www.facebook.com/hypnotherapysoutheast, and please do join the Facebook Group 'Weight off Your Plate' for more tips!

Printed in Poland
by Amazon Fulfillment
Poland Sp. z o.o., Wrocław

53451258R00063